Praise for *Four Secrets to Liking Your Work*

"I wish I had this book when I started teaching! It's a must-read for anybody who works. The simple, organized, and realistic exercises gave me new perspective about who I am, and helped me learn to better enjoy what I do."

—**Krystal Wood, Elementary School Educator**

"A must read! With a hands-on approach and actual homework activities, it will change your whole outlook and give you the fresh start you need. The light at the end of the tunnel is no longer a train, but the bright future of a renewed and refreshed perspective."

—**Robert H. Mallory, Accredited Green Building Professional, Southwest Noise Control, LLC**

"There are many guides to finding the right job out there, but few others teach us to make the most of our current situation. The understanding of self and others taught in this book will help people to be at their most constructive, whether they are working at home or in a more traditional environment."

—**Anne Laird, Homemaker & Small Business Owner**

"Helped me understand what drives me and, more importantly, what drives the people I love and work with. This book will help anyone communicate more effectively, improve relationships, and reduce the pain they feel at work."

—**Joseph Rodman, Director of Training and Education, Jaynes Construction**

"Working with others is unavoidable; this book gives you a deeper understanding of what makes them tick. It's a concise, easy read that will improve your personal and professional life."

—**Dr. Donald E. Conklin, Vice President, United Corporate Services, Inc., and Adjunct Professor, Dominican College MBA Program**

"Proactive and empowering! How I wish I had *Four Secrets to Liking Your Work* during the times my work as a Pastor was not only frustrating, but also depleting me emotionally and spiritually! The book is full of practical tools and approaches that help reverse the downward spiral that we face when we're unhappy at work. It puts the control back in our own hands, and helps us to create work lives that are happier and even emotionally and spiritually enriching. I strongly recommend *Four Secrets to Liking Your Work* to anyone who is experiencing difficulty in his or her work life."

—**The Rev. Dr. Paul Debenport, Senior Pastor, and Head of Staff, First Presbyterian Church of Albuquerque**

D0951674

"Life is too short to not enjoy what you do! This book is a gem, filled with practical, simple, and direct advice for untangling the twisted nets of communication failures. It is as valuable to an employer trying to maintain high-functioning teams as it is to an employee who is feeling dissatisfied."

—R.A. Bobbi Hayes, CPA, Partner, Accounting & Consulting Group, LLP

"By internalizing the mind-expanding principles presented in *Four Secrets to Liking Your Work*, I am now enjoying my work on a much deeper level. Many times when I thought my coworkers simply 'weren't getting it,' it was actually *I* who wasn't getting it! There is no empty feel-good rhetoric here—this book distinguishes itself from pop self-improvement books by focusing on breaking through barriers with disciplined action instead of just giving you a pep talk. It provides the missing tools everybody needs."

—Jim Foster, Vice President, Staffing and Human Capital

"Liking your work is one of the greatest blessings in life, and these authors know all about how to find or create that blessing. Those who follow this book's advice will see lights turn on wherever they are in the world of work.

Leaders, listen up! This book is not just about you, but about everyone you work with. HR, listen up! This book will help with on-boarding AND with retention."

—William R. Daniels, CEO, American Consulting & Training, and Author, *Breakthrough Performance* and *Change-Able Organization*

"In a globalized world, this book provides analytical tools and approaches for honoring differences in the workplace."

—Ron Sacchi, Director of Organizational Learning and Development, VeriSign, Inc., and Author, *Design/Build Your Business*

"A gem of a book for anyone who works with or manages others. Provides insights and exercises that reveal the secrets you need to enjoy your work and your successes."

—Dion McInnis, University Administrator, and Author, *Listen to Life, Wisdom in Life's Stories*

"I have known just one or two of the *Four Secrets to Liking Your Work*, when used individually, to enable leaders to maximize productivity, and to make a huge difference in how teams operate. In combination, the Secrets have the potential to be one of the most powerful team building and organizational assessment tools I have ever seen."

—Steve Overcashier, OD and Training Manager, COPART Inc., (#140 of the FORBES 200 Best Small Companies)

"The logical next step to the *Strengths Finder*, and an enjoyable read."

—Lisa Baker, Vice President of Marketing, Hewlett-Packard

"Provides pragmatic ways of developing self-awareness and using it to take your career in powerful new directions. Anyone can use the four Secrets to find career happiness and ongoing success."

—Gail Hurt, CEO, Living Authentically Career & Life Mentoring, Certified Career Practitioner

"A no-nonsense, practical guide to dispassionately evaluate job dissatisfaction *and* an invaluable framework for evaluating human interactions far beyond the workplace. Clear and relevant, with analogies, examples, and a tinge of humor. An accessible and exceedingly useful tool.

Dissatisfied employees who are wondering whether they should leave their jobs owe it to themselves to read this book and move toward a better future at work— whether they choose to leave or stay."

—Janet Williams, Site Strategy Manager, Atomic Weapons Establishment (England)

"An inspiration and a relief! I've seen many tools, but none that approach things as effectively as this book does. It will do a lot of good for a lot of people."

—Peggy Robinson, Senior Education Coordinator, 3M (Retired)

"Because we aren't taught about office relationships in law school, our actual experiences can be so negative as to drive us away from our hard-earned careers. This book is the needed prescription for dealing with a sour and enervating workplace, teaching us what our formal educations ignored, and putting us on the road to a more rewarding experience in our workplaces."

—Denise D. Fort, Professor of Law

"Taken together, the four Secrets create a powerful environment for change. Although the book is written at higher level than others, it does a great job explaining and simplifying complex concepts."

—Lynne H. Schluter, Manager, Facilities SMU Partnerships, Lockheed

"An easy read, different from what I have read in the past. Provides tools for in-depth understanding which allow the reader to make better choices at work."

—Gerald Lipka, Corporate Project Manager, Sandia National Laboratories

"Wow! What a great book! It connects so many career and life lessons like puzzle pieces, and makes them all fit together at work."

—Denise Schultze, Central NM President, National Membership Chair, Society of Women Engineers

"The ideas in this book really opened my eyes and taught me the skills I needed to discover my own needs and desires for a satisfying job experience."

—Ellen Phifer, Technical Team Lead, SURVICE Engineering

"Packed with practical, useful information. Like reading a book about people I know."

—Laura Oliphant, PhD, Senior Investment Manager, Intel Capital

"Presents concepts that are both useful and thought-provoking. A reference manual and a very useful tool."

—Dave Berry, Senior Systems Engineer, Harris County

"Truly enjoyable! The most fun I've had with a career tool ever! Information presented in a new and very usable way; skills everyone should know and use. I'd give a copy to everyone on my team!"

—Bernice Brody, PMP, Executive Project Manager, IBM

Four
Secrets
to Liking
Your Work

Four Secrets to Liking Your Work

You May Not Need to Quit to Get the Job You Want

Edward G. Muzio | Deborah J. Fisher, PhD | Erv Thomas, PE

Vice President, Publisher: Tim Moore
Associate Publisher and Director of Marketing: Amy Neidlinger
Acquisitions Editor: Jennifer Simon
Editorial Assistant: Pamela Boland
Digital Marketing Manager: Julie Phifer
Publicist: Amy Fandrei
Development Editor: Russ Hall
Cover Designer: Sandra Schroeder
Managing Editor: Gina Kanouse
Senior Project Editor: Kristy Hart
Copy Editor: Language Logistics, LLC
Proofreader: Williams Woods Publishing Services, LLC
Senior Indexer: Cheryl Lenser
Interior Designer/Senior Compositor: Gloria Schurick
Manufacturing Buyer: Dan Uhrig

© 2008 by Pearson Education, Inc.
Publishing as FT Press
Upper Saddle River, New Jersey 07458

FT Press offers excellent discounts on this book when ordered in quantity for bulk purchases
or special sales. For more information, please contact U.S. Corporate and Government Sales,
1-800-382-3419, corpsales@pearsontechgroup.com. For sales outside the U.S., please contact
International Sales at international@pearsoned.com.

Printed in the United States of America

23 24 25 26 27 28 29 30 V036 18 17 16 15

ISBN-10: 0-13-234445-9
ISBN-13: 978-0-13-234445-6

Pearson Education LTD.
Pearson Education Australia PTY, Limited.
Pearson Education Singapore, Pte. Ltd.
Pearson Education North Asia, Ltd.
Pearson Education Canada, Ltd.
Pearson Educatión de Mexico, S.A. de C.V.
Pearson Education—Japan
Pearson Education Malaysia, Pte. Ltd.

Library of Congress Cataloging-in-Publication Data

Muzio, Edward G. (Edward Gregory), 1974-

   Four secrets to liking your work : you may not need to quit to get the job you want / Edward
G. Muzio, Deborah J. Fisher, Erv Thomas.

      p. cm.

   ISBN 0-13-234445-9 (hardback : alk. paper) 1. Organizational behavior. 2. Work—
Psychological aspects. 3. Motivation (Psychology) 4. Interpersonal relations. 5. Self-
management (Psychology) I. Fisher, Deborah J. (Deborah Jansen), 1951 Apr. 11- II. Thomas,
Erv, 1958- III. Title.

   HD58.7.M89 2007

   650.1--dc22

                                    2007028650

This product is printed digitally on demand.

This book is dedicated to all the workers
still clinging to the hope that it can get better.

Contents

CONTENTS

Acknowledgments

First, we are indebted to our significant others, who not only tolerated the time this book took from away from them, but also gave freely of their own time, advice, and support.

Next, we cannot offer enough thanks to our initial editorial staff, Jennifer Simon, Russ Hall, Kristy Hart, and to the rest of the team at FT Press. All of them together helped us turn our ideas into something that others can access, understand, and put to good use.

Finally, we are grateful for the individuals, employers, and environments that have provided the opportunities to learn all that we know about this material. Chief among them are Intel Corporation, The University of New Mexico, Target Training International, Mr. J. Michael Bown, and Group Harmonics.

—*Ed Muzio, "Dr. Deb" Fisher, and Erv Thomas*

About the Authors

Edward G. Muzio is President and CEO of Group Harmonics and a leader in the application of analytical models to enhance group effectiveness. He has started large organizations and small companies, led global initiatives in technology development and employee recruitment, and published papers ranging from manufacturing strategy to individual skills and productivity. As primary developer of his company's educational suite, he serves as advisor and educator to workers at all levels in companies worldwide.

Deborah J. Fisher, PhD is a Visiting Research Professor at the University of New Mexico. Dedicated to group productivity and human motivation, her career has included tenure and an endowed chair position at her current institution, and Directorship of the Engineering Management Program at the University of Houston. She has automated organizational learning for the construction industry, created employee development models for Sandia National Laboratories, and educated generations of professionals along the way.

Erv Thomas, PE is a Program Manager at Intel Corporation. For the past several years he has been responsible for recruiting, mentoring, and developing the top engineering talent in the world. He has dedicated over 30,000 hours of his time to helping professionals and young adults live up to their full potential at work and in life. Additionally, he has been a design engineer, an educator, and the founding director of a non-profit organization where he has spent the majority of his "non-working" time mentoring teens at risk.

Monday Morning Dread

The alarm broke the peaceful silence of the bedroom with an ugly metallic buzz, the dial glowing sallow green numerals of an obscene hour. Brian rubbed his eyes; consciousness came slowly. Soon, that old feeling of "work dread" began to smother his spirit. The day ahead of him drifted into focus, and his all too familiar feeling of dismay was close behind: It's time to go to work.

Like many, Brian lost his "will to work" years ago. The thought of a whole week at "that place" made him want to go back to sleep or to vanish and never return. The conflict, the oppression, the sadness, and the boredom were unbearable. Yet he could find no alternative. Bills needed to be paid, and he had become fond of eating.

Old habits die hard. Brian had dreaded his job for so long, it was the first thing he thought of as he awoke. But then he remembered something else. Six months ago, he had been given a book, one that claimed he could like his job again. It explained different ways of looking at work, through filters or lenses that could help to identify some of the dread and replace it with action. "One kind of Genius," the authors claimed, "is the ability to see the same situation from multiple perspectives."[1] Changed understanding can produce changed action; changed action produces changed results. He was utterly skeptical, but he had no better option. He read his new book and waited for failure.

To his surprise, it helped. It wasn't long before he felt a small shift. This made him just a little less skeptical. The more he used the book, the better it worked. His job became first more tolerable, then more enjoyable. When he had started reading, he had been intent upon quitting his job as soon as possible. Now, he wasn't sure. Maybe it wasn't so bad if he approached it the right way. This was a novel thought for Brian.

As he awakened that Monday morning, Brian felt the familiar dread and then remembered his new strategy. "What am I dreading," he wondered? He recalled that often it is a single, fixable problem that overshadows everything else. Several difficult things were going to happen that day, but which one was causing the dread? One by one, he tried the different perspectives taught by the book, isolating each possible source of his pain.

He found it. He would have to work with a particularly troublesome person that afternoon, someone he would otherwise avoid. In his mind's eye, he looked again at that interaction with his new perspective. He considered what would probably happen and planned his responses accordingly. He knew things wouldn't be perfect, but he decided he could at least make a slight improvement.

He checked, and his feeling of dread had vanished.

Welcome to Brian's book.

Why Do We Work?

Besides the obvious answer, "to survive," there are deeper, more meaningful reasons to work. The idea of applying our energy to create a positive result is fundamental to both our culture and our belief systems.

The ideal of "the value of hard work" is culturally pervasive, from the children's story of "The Little Engine That Could"[2] to the iconic account of a person of modest background who works hard and "makes good." One need not be from the United States. Otherwise privileged students at the People's University of China, for example, work in service-oriented jobs for educational credit. Why? To learn the value of working hard and efficiently, a value espoused by Chinese President Hu Jintao.[3]

This value runs deeper, to our spiritual beliefs. A large number of creation accounts have existed, from ancient times to present, describing a creator working to construct the world as we know it.[4] From the Japanese account of gods Izanagi and Izanami[5] fashioning the world from chaos, to the Iroquois (Native American) account of animal spirits creating terra firma with mud from the bottom of the sea,[6] to the Judeo-Christian account of God creating the world in six days and stating "it is good[7]," faith traditions abound that discreetly reinforce the link between work and positive outcome at the highest level.

Work at Its Best

Whether it is a spiritual account of a creator at work in the heavens, an iconic literary figure turning gumption to payoff, or an employee spending energy to produce a result and receive a paycheck, work is the application of effort to add value to the world. We have no shortage of problems; opportunities abound for us to contribute however we can. Through work, we become "part of the solution" rather than "part of the problem." Whether you are working on the cure for cancer, grilling burgers for hungry customers, or laboring at home to raise your children, you are contributing positive results to the world.

Work validates our own sense of value and contribution and gives us a sense of identity. For many, work is where we spend most of our time; it becomes the backdrop against which we define ourselves—so much so, in fact, that many of us don't want to leave. There are more than 4.5 million members of the workforce today who retired and then began working again because they "wanted to." This group's motivation was not financial; instead, they listed reasons such as health, energy, and fun for returning to the workplace.[8] Work adds value to us even as we add value to the world.

As we grow and develop in the context of work, it forces us to look inward and understand who we really are: our gifts, talents, weaknesses, and passions. Work can support us at multiple levels of development, from building physiological safety and security to learning self-esteem. Over the years, it becomes the canvas on which we self-actualize.[9] So many of us have individual accounts of how we learned and grew individually from experiences at work.

At its best, work can help us learn patience, understanding, humility, empathy, constructive confrontation, honesty, and integrity. The lessons and skills that make us more effective at work can also make us more effective in life. Ideally our work should bring us joy.

Work at Its Worst

The reality is often the opposite. Work can produce negative results. It can be used to cheat, to lie and to hurt other people. Much "work" was done within World War II and the holocaust, for example. Work can tear down others, even those we love. It can hinder the progress of others simply to make someone look better, and working energy can be spent to cover up wrongdoing. We can even work hard at pretending to work!

Work can build us up, but it can also tear us down. It can involve long hours over an extended period and physical and emotional stress. Many of us have experienced negative workplaces that demean employees, either accidentally or intentionally. This has a tremendous impact on self-esteem, productivity, and morale. Many people come to feel devalued, insecure, and discouraged because of the environment in which they work. They get no feeling of pride, accomplishment, or value from working.

Some of this is not directly in our control; we can't "stop" an environment from being difficult. On the other hand, downtrodden employees often have more capability, resources, and options at hand than they realize. We cannot choose the actions of others, but we are always free to choose how we interpret and process them. In those choices lie chances to grow.

What Work Offers

You might simply feel as if you have to work to survive, and all you want to do is experience less dread and misery. If so, this book can help you achieve that goal. If you've been suffering for a long time, "less dread" in itself may seem to be an ideal or unreachable goal.

We hope that you will consider another goal for work. Work teaches us much about ourselves. Some of the most useful pieces of information are the *reasons* behind our satisfaction or misery. Viewed carefully, those reasons act like mirrors, showing us hidden facets of our strengths and preferences. How carefully we gather that knowledge and what we do with it is entirely up to us. This book isn't only about "suffering less." It's also about "learning more"—that is, learning more about ourselves, more about those around us, and more about how to find or create the environment we need to thrive. We can build on our knowledge and let it direct our paths into the future.

There is, of course, a risk. With knowledge of our strengths comes knowledge of our weaknesses. As we learn, we must use the knowledge we gather *for* ourselves, not *against* ourselves. Rather than being proud of our abilities, it is easy to become depressed about what we lack. But if we focus on our weaknesses and ignore our strengths, our greatest gifts lie dormant and undeveloped, and we become weaker still.[10] The goal—of this book and at work—is not to harp on weaknesses, but to find a way to play to our strengths as often as possible.[11]

How Far Could You Go if You Loved Your Job?

Imagine a work life so compelling that winning the lottery would change your bank account balance but not your daily routine.

How would this type of joy and balance affect your life? How far could you go? How much money could you make? How much could you learn? How well could you support your loved ones? What could you contribute to the world? What could you contribute to yourself?

Imagine living and working like this for 10 years. How about 20, 30, 40 years? Now imagine looking back on all of this productive, joyful work. What will you have accomplished?

This book is not a stop-whining-fast program inflicted *on* you by someone else. It is about you *doing* what you can to make your work life better. Imagine for a minute that you looked forward to Monday morning. Imagine work that was fun, engaging, and felt more like recreation and less like…well, work! Imagine thinking, "I can't believe I get paid for this."

It's hard to believe that a conscientious worker would not also be a successful one in such a situation.[12] It might sound like a naïve and impossible goal if you're in the majority, dissatisfied with your job and feeling trapped, but it is possible to achieve this kind of satisfaction. And like any object of pursuit, your odds of success increase tremendously when you understand what "it" is and what "it" looks like.

So let's begin…

chapter one

The Trouble with Work

"It's just another manic Monday."
—The Bangles[1]

You dread, dislike, or even hate your job, but you are going anyway. What else can you do?

You could take drugs. Prescription anti-depressants are on the rise,[2] and disgruntled employees are surprisingly forthright in claims that they need the pills to make it through the week. And then there are other drugs, obtained without a prescription, and less likely to be mentioned.

You could "get a spouse who complains a lot and have a few kids." This suggestion comes from a Dilbert character who suggests making work better by turning it into the lesser of two evils.[3] The same approach might work equally well using inconsiderate roommates or a leaky roof in a rainy climate. No matter how bad work is, just make home even worse.

Suicide, of course, is not the answer. Yet some studies have suggested that the highest suicide rate occurs on Monday.[4] The more you hear how people feel about their jobs, the easier this surprising statistic becomes to believe.

Is that it? Drugs, suffering, and death seem like poor alternatives. There must be a better way that is not illegal, expensive, or quite so drastic.

Do We All Hate Our Jobs?

Picture a room filled with ten of your coworkers. Odds are that seven of them don't like what they do.[5] Do you know which ones? Are you one of them?

It gets worse. Research suggests that one of those seven coworkers might be actively working at cross purposes to undermine your company. This means that if you are trying to be productive, he or she is working against you, too![6]

Why bother working at all? We like to believe that it's all about the money. We see people endure dread, dissatisfaction, and misery in the name of the paycheck, but Herzberg and Maslow agree that once our monetary needs are met, it ceases to motivate us.[7] And even if we do need the money, it's no substitute for engaging, enjoyable, productive work. Money can't buy back lost time.

The People Problem

Are you stressed?

The rate of workers calling in due to stress-related illness has been rising for years, and stressed workers have about twice the absentee rate of non-stressed workers.[8] People problems cause stress, and stress causes dread. Both are on the rise.

Why? Survey after survey indicates that human issues are what really drive dissatisfaction. "Boss" and "coworkers" appear prominently in every study and anecdote of workplace stressors. "Conflict," "confusion," "tension," and "poor leadership" round out the picture. Even initial reports that "I don't like the work" often lead to deeper issues of absent advancement opportunity or misalignment of skills, shifting the real cause back to the human issues.[9]

People problems kill productivity. Experts agree that the majority of lost productivity is due to employees who show up for work but don't really engage.[10] The price tag to employers is estimated at $300 billion per year for the lost productivity associated with disengagement![11] That much money is hard to fathom, but it's not hard to believe. Anyone who has worked with other people has war stories about the damage caused by those who just don't care.

The Personal Cost

At the end of the day, it's not about your company or your boss. It's about you!

Those of us who work full time spend about half our waking hours working. This is the half in which we are at our most awake, most productive, and most attentive. Add the time we spend getting ready for work, commuting, and thinking about our jobs, and we see that we are using the majority of our lives to work. It had better be work we like!

Job-related misery robs us of our best, most productive days and years. It increases stress and illness, causes fatigue, shortens life, ends marriages, separates families, and destroys quality of life.

Job misery costs the employer a lot, but it costs the employee everything.

The Beginning

Venting

If you're reading this book, there are at least a few things about your job that you don't like. If you're like a lot of people, there are more than just a few. Before we start trying to change these things or even to understand them, it's important to get "all the cards on the table." So let's get specific. Find yourself a blank sheet of paper, a quiet corner, and get ready to vent!

Here's how: Draw a vertical line down the center of the sheet of paper. On the left side, write the word "PROBLEMS" at the top. Underneath, make a list of all of the things about your job that bother you. Anything goes! You can be specific or vague, listing people, places, tasks, relationships, or anything else. The only rules for your list are to leave at least two lines of space between each item on the list and to use only the left hand side of the page. Start as many new pages as you need to make the list complete; just follow the same format on each page (see Figure 1-1).

After that's done, it's time to get even more specific. Write the word "EVIDENCE" at the top of the right side. To the right of each of the problems you listed, write a few comments about how you know that the problem is happening. Imagine that your whole work day was videotaped and that you want to explain the worst parts of your job to a close friend watching the tape. What would you point out to illustrate the problem(s)?

You might not be able to provide evidence for everything on your list. Do your best but don't worry if you can't think of evidence for some of your problems.

When your list is complete, read it once. This is the core of your job dread. Some items might be solvable, others might be permanent, but all of them together comprise the source of your negative experience at work.

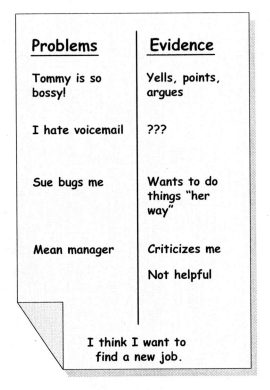

Figure 1-1 *Sample problems and evidence "venting" list*

Should I Stay or Should I Go?

Your list might be short, or it might be long. If you've hated your job for a long time, you are probably pretty sure you want to leave. If not, you might want to fix things, or you might simply be unsure what to do next. Choose one of the following three sentences and write it at the bottom of the last page of your list:

- I think I want to find a new job.
- I think I want to stay in this job.
- I'm not sure whether to stay or leave.

Either option might turn out to be the best answer for you. A big part of the value of the new perspectives you will learn in this book is that they will help you decide.

For now, fold up your list and seal it in an envelope. We mean this literally: Don't just fold the flap, but seal the envelope as if you were going to mail it. Label the envelope "FOR LATER" and store it safely. We *will* return to this list and this question. For now, we are literally and figuratively setting these things aside so that we can practice with some new perspectives.

Seeing Differently Through Models

As the old adage goes, if you don't like your situation, you have three options: Accept it, leave it, or change it. If you are reading this book, you have been "accepting" a poor situation for too long and are ready to try another option. But which one?

Change the Situation

Can you fix things where you are? Job dissatisfaction creates a vicious downward cycle leading to apathy and disengagement. As the adverse conditions pile on, the disgruntled worker retreats into a world of detachment and unhappiness. Many can't even put words around what the problems are. Others honestly would like to make things better but believe they can't or don't know where to begin—and don't even try. Will anything work?

Leave the Situation

Can you find somewhere better? Perhaps the situation at your current job is beyond repair. Those of us seeking new employment would probably agree. But if more than three quarters of us say that things are better elsewhere,[12] *where is elsewhere*? Can it be that the grass really is greener for *me* on *your* side, and vice-versa? How do we know what to look for?

First, Change Your Perspective

Are you being driven crazy at work by people who are pushy? Flaky? Lazy? Stupid? Consider a fourth option: Before "accepting them, changing them, or leaving them," try changing your perspective. This is the best first step before you make the other changes.

What if you're sure you need a new job? That's fine; the first step is still the same. By using new perspectives to see your current situation, you build skills that go with you to your next position and every position after that. More importantly, the skills help you with your job hunt!

There is no worse time to look for a new job than when you hate the one you have. The "Any Port in a Storm" syndrome makes even the worst option attractive. Your new perspectives will allow you instead to evaluate your options based on your needs and avoid making a change for the worse.

You've tried accepting it. Whatever you try next—changing it, leaving it, or just looking at it differently, the perspective change must come first. Otherwise, the actions you take might lead to a worse situation than you are in now.

The Magic of Perspective

Glasses without Frames

It sounds too easy. "Change your perspective, change your job." Could it be so simple?

When we have hated our jobs for long enough, it starts to seem impossible to fix things. Every day we see evidence why our workplace is awful; after awhile this becomes just a part of "how things are." To suggest that it would be possible to change it by merely looking at it differently sounds naïve and ridiculous!

On the other hand, what we call "reality" is defined by our perception of it. Our eyes and ears assemble information, and our brain processes it. Along the way, the "objective" information that we are processing gets entangled with our subjective selves. Our history, our biases, our preferences, and our emotions all come into play as we make our assessment of what is "real." Some information gets emphasized, some gets filtered out, and what we are left with is our own perception of reality. This version contains both the situation and the self.

However you feel about your job, there will be parts of it that grab your attention and parts that don't. The parts that grab your attention are the ones you respond to; they are the ones you use to craft your definition of "how things are" and decide how to respond. The other parts, filtered out along the way, just drop into the background of your perceptions.

A change in perspective can make all the difference. Consider "polarized" sunglasses, a favorite among fishermen because they eliminate glare from the surface of the water. Imagine standing at the edge of a fishing boat, looking down at the water and seeing nothing but reflected sunlight. Do you cast your line here or move on to a different location? The answer is pure guesswork.

Imagine donning a pair of polarized lenses. The glare disappears; you can see 30 feet into the water. Now you know what swims beneath you. Guesswork is gone, along with the stress that goes with it. Your responses are more closely matched to your situation, and your sense of uncertainty decreases. Over time, your overall sense of "how hard it is to fish" probably decreases too.

If you can find a new perspective, then you're more likely to choose a different response. If your new perspective gives you new clarity, your different response might be a better and more productive one. And each different response can produce a different outcome. If you use your new perspective enough times and create enough different outcomes, suddenly your whole experience of the situation has changed.

Cultural author and columnist Tamim Ansary said this about glasses:

Eyeglasses that corrected both nearsightedness and farsightedness [became available] around 1450...I have an affliction that is considered trivial today: I'm myopic. If I were living before eyeglasses, I would be considered blind. My job would be to sit by a road with a begging cup. Roughly 25 percent of the people in North America are nearsighted like me. I wonder how many potential writers, artists, scientists, inventors, philosophers, and the like never developed their talents because they lived before the invention of eyeglasses?[13]

Each new perspective we try is a new pair of glasses. The situation doesn't change, but the way we see it does. Some elements become clearer and more pronounced while others fade into the background. Things that took up our whole field of view become less important.

As any eye doctor will tell you, there's no way to know for sure whether the new glasses will be useful without trying them on, but the right pair can change everything.

Wearing New Glasses

New perspectives give us new options, especially in difficult situations or those where the stakes are high. Like polarized lenses for the fisherman, a useful change in our own perspective will reveal hidden information; it will make us "situationally smarter!" The more we know about a situation, the better equipped we are to respond to it. We think of options that we hadn't before because we have a more complete view of what is going on.

This has positive effects on our self-confidence and our stress level. There are few things more frustrating for a fisherman than to cast all day based on guesswork and to go home empty-handed. By the same token...

...There are few things more frustrating than to work all day at the whim of our situation, battered about by forces that seem random, and then to go home exhausted and depleted.

If instead we understand what's going on, respond accordingly, and know when to expect the next wave of trouble to hit, things are better. We might still be tired at the end of the day, but we will be a lot less stressed.

Our own feeling of increased control and decreased stress has an important side effect: It reduces the stress levels of those around us. Studies have shown that only a few people in a large group are needed to change the dynamics and tension levels of everyone around them.[14] Most of us have experienced this phenomenon in the negative direction, with "one rotten apple spoiling the whole bunch." But it goes both ways! By reducing your own stress levels, your mere presence can reduce the stress of those around you. Wouldn't it be nice to be surrounded by people who are even just a little less stressed?

Changing Perspective: An Exercise

Our first activity in changing perspective is simple but powerful. On first read, it also seems quite silly. But rest assured, it is based upon the empirical science of how the mind works.[15] What seem like childish or unnecessary exercises are actually physical cues to activate specific parts of your mind. The difference between *reading* this exercise and *doing* it is the difference between *wanting* things to get better at work and *making* them get better. It sets the stage for all that you will be doing in future chapters. It can also be fun. We suggest, therefore, that you begin your experience with this book by setting aside any cynicism you might feel and trying this out as fully as you can.

You will need three sheets of blank paper to begin. Number the pages 1 through 3 by writing a large number on each that takes up the entire page. Set the three pages face up on the floor a few feet from each other so that they form a triangle.

Think of a situation in which you've had a disagreement with another person. Choose an instance you remember well. Recall who was involved and the object of the conflict.

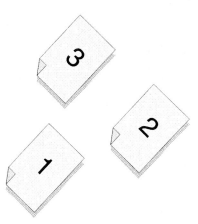

Figure 1-2 *The three sheet exercise*

Now step onto the sheet labeled "1." Stand [16] with both feet on the sheet, facing sheet 2. This is the first person position because you are "being yourself." The person with whom you disagree is the "second person." Imagine that he or she is standing on sheet 2 and that you are having the conflict you remember. Explain your position out loud as if you are speaking to the other person. You can also pause and make "aside" statements about what you are thinking or feeling that are not meant for the second person to hear. Keep talking until you feel that you have explained your position as fully as possible.

Then step off of sheet 1 and on to sheet 2. Turn so that you are facing sheet 1. Now you are in the second person position. Imagine that you *are* that other person. As you look over at sheet 1, try to picture *yourself* standing on it, arguing your position. See yourself from the other person's perspective! As long as you are on sheet 2, your role is to be the best "other person" you can be. Work hard to play the role of the other person as well as you can. Have the conflict again, this time as the other person. Speak *as* the second person and argue *with* the first person. What are your needs, wants, and feelings? Again, you might want to say some things within the conflict and make other "aside" comments not meant to be heard. Both are useful.

It is important to resist the temptation to "play" the other person as being stupid, confused, or misinformed—especially if that is how he or she appeared to you in the original conflict. To get value out of this exercise, you must act out the other person's role as a rational, intelligent human being, no matter how difficult this might be. Try to be the best, brightest, most thoughtful second person you can be. In doing so, you might feel as if you are giving the other person "too much credit." That is a good sign. The aim is not to prove anyone right or wrong; it is to give you practice with changed perspectives.

Then step on to sheet 3. Stand so that you are facing sheets 1 and 2 equally. In the third person position, you are an observer of the interaction, a neutral party who sees everything that is going on but doesn't care how the argument turns out. This is the "fly on the wall" position. Imagine now that you can see both yourself (on sheet 1) and the other person (on sheet 2) as the interaction happens between them. Try to view both parties as acquaintances so that you have a general interest in seeing what happens without a preference for either side's position.

Watch the conflict play out, with each side stating their positions and arguing with the other. What do you see? Picture the interaction as completely as you can. Think about voice tone, body language, posture, hand gestures. How long did it take? How heated did it get? At the end, how were things left? How did each person appear to feel as the conflict came to a close? Is there anything you can see that the two people in conflict cannot? Describe what you see aloud, as if you were the narrator of a story or the announcer at a boxing match. As you narrate, use your right forefinger to repeatedly tap the inside of your left palm at the base of your left thumb, once every few seconds. Continue narrating and tapping until you have described the situation to your satisfaction.

Tapping your palm like this provides a physical "anchor" to help keep you in the third person position.

At this point, you will have experienced the same conflict three times from three different perspectives. Most people find that they "see" something different with each new perspective. Often participants in this exercise report that they leave with a better understanding of the real reason for the conflict and perhaps even a little more empathy for the other person's position. Take a moment to answer this question: If there were three things you learned from doing this exercise, what would they be?

About Perspective Shift

It takes a lot of effort to look at your sunglasses while you are wearing them. The same is true about shifting perspective. To adjust the "lenses" through which we view the world, we must first become aware of them.

New perspective shifts require well-defined models.

10

Imagine if, in place of the detailed instructions for the three-sheet exercise, this book had simply instructed you to "think of a recent conflict and then try to see it from the other person's position and like a fly on the wall." Those instructions are technically correct, but in the absence of a clear process and steps to follow, most of us probably would have not learned nearly as much about the situation.

Why? Many of us don't have much experience with *how* to change perceptual positions. By requiring us to step on and off of sheets of paper and to imagine the other people in the situation, the three-sheet model provides a framework to help develop our new perspective. At the same time, it alerts our minds that a shift is coming. Like training wheels for a new bicyclist, the model provides help and support while we learn a new skill.

If you repeat the three-sheet exercise many times, eventually you will become quite adept at switching positions. At that point, your high level of expertise will replace your need for the exercise, and you will no longer need sheets of paper to switch perceptual positions. That's when "the training wheels come off."

The upcoming chapters of this book present specific perspectives to help you see new things in the same situations. Each new perspective comes with its own model, a framework to support you while you learn to see things in the "new" way. And each new perspective, when used carefully, will give you new insight into what is going on around you at work. Your new insight will lead you to new actions, and your new actions might very well change your experience of your job. At the very least, they will teach you what to look for in your next job.

Unlike the three-sheet exercise, the chapters to come will not require you to pretend you are someone else, but they will require you to see things from the "third person." The ability to mentally "step out of" your own role and into an observer role is crucial; as long as you are "stuck" in the first person, your ability to perceive things differently is severely limited. Stepping into the third person position and looking at what is happening with an objective eye is the beginning of any major perspective shift.

Author and professional athlete Arthur Ashe said that "Success is a journey, not a destination. The doing is more important than the outcome." The same is true here; if you focus on the doing, the outcome follows naturally. As with any sport, you start learning by getting used to the movements. The fun and the good results follow, and they increase along the way.

Tips for the Journey

If one definition of "genius" is the ability to see the same situation from multiple perspectives,[17] then this book is a guide to becoming a workplace genius. Some ideas will work right away; others will take more time. All of them will require you to first *learn from* the situation and then *take action* based on what you learn.

While you are learning and taking action, keep in mind the following tips:

Stay Employed

As you try to make your job better or to find your way to a better job, be sure to keep doing your current job to the best of your ability. Choose actions that will help and not hinder your level of success. Even if you are planning on quitting, doing a good job on the way out can only help you down the road.

Stay Engaged

This book is a blend of description and exercise. The descriptions will help you to understand new ways of thinking, but you will only get the full benefit if you try out the exercises. Without jeopardizing your career, do all of the exercises as completely as you can. You'll be surprised by the results!

Be Supported

Changes in perspective are changes in how we think about things. They can be complicated, and they might require us to change our habits. One way to make great progress through this book is to find one or more other people who are will-ing to talk with you about your progress, or better yet who are working through the book themselves! A friend, mentor, or study group can help you to stay on course and be a valuable source of discussion and support. Find someone who will hold you accountable! You can visit www.likeworkagain.com/support for ideas and resources.

Be Selective

It's important to find support and equally important to be discriminating in where you look for it. Choose your advisors carefully! Telling a difficult boss that you are about to try out a new strategy on her, for example, might be a setup for failure. What you learn in this book is like learning a new language: You can think in it at any time, but you should only speak it with others who can understand and reciprocate immediately or who are willing to listen and learn.

Drive the Change

Our beliefs and our actions are partners in our experience; we can change either one by changing the other. You might not believe it is possible for you to like your job again, and you might be skeptical that anything can help. That's fine, but for the purposes of this book, it's best to act as if you think change is possible. That way, if it turns out that it is possible, you won't miss the opportunity to make the change. Who knows, you might come to a different set of beliefs as a result of your actions.

Own the Wins

If you follow through on what this book suggests, there will be times when you experience good results. Some will be small, like an interaction with a troublesome coworker that goes "just a little bit better." Some might be bigger, like winning the day by influencing someone important. It is critical that you take ownership of your successes, small and large. They are a result of *your* efforts. Don't attribute them to luck or chance; take credit! This will help you build confidence in your new skills for the next time you need them.

Stay Positive

Not every situation will be a win. You will have moments where you "forget" what you are learning, and it might feel as if you are going backwards. You might get caught up in the moment and fall back into old habits. You might try things that don't work,[18] or you might forget to try anything at all. This is part of the process. It sounds cliché, but setbacks provide the chance to learn something new. Every step might not bring you closer to your goal, but all of your steps taken together will. Don't get discouraged!

Read the Stories

You will find a variety of stories in this book. While the names and details in some of the stories have been altered, they are all based on real situations. Often stories provide a great way to learn and think about new concepts.[19] That's partly because stories give us a chance to relate ideas to our own experience. So whenever you are reading a "true story" from this book, consider whether you or someone you know has had any similar experiences.

Do the Work

This book contains a number of interactive exercises. The more you apply this book to your situation, the more useful it will be. If you are struggling with a particular model or it is your first time through the book, you can start with the beginner-level exercises. As you get more comfortable with a given perspective, or if you decide to reread the book again, you can move into the more advanced exercises. Just remember this:

Perspective shifting exercises are like physical exercises:
Some are easier, some are harder. To get the full benefit of working out,
you have to do them all!

Get Organized

We suggest you obtain a small notebook for your thoughts and responses to activities. Even if you're not inclined to write in great detail, it can be useful to take just a few notes in each section while you learn and experiment with each new perspective. Your notes will be especially helpful when you reach the end of the book and revisit your list of what's wrong in your job today.

If you are able to carry the notebook with you to work, you can make entries there and then reflect on them back at home. As you try new responses based on your new perceptions, you can make notes about what works. Like a scientist, you can study your workplace from the third-person position and determine through experimentation how to influence your environment.

"Rinse and Repeat"

There's one other tool that is essential whenever you learn something new: practice. The purpose of this book is to teach you the skills to regain a positive work experience. They only work if you use them, and "practice makes perfect." Nobody ever learned to ride a bicycle just by reading the instruction manual that came with it. Eventually, you have to get on, pedal, fall a few times, and keep trying until you find your balance. The same is true here: don't be afraid to repeat an exercise, a chapter, or even the whole book!

Homework: Before, During, and After

Each section of this book ends with three kinds of homework: before work, during work, and after work. The intent is for you to try each perspective or set of tools at your workplace. In this section, you observe what goes on and prepare for the perspective shifts in future chapters.

Before Work

Before going to work, take the following actions:

1. Find a tablet or pad that you can use as a *Like Work Again* notebook. It is best to use one in which pages aren't easily removed. The intent is to keep your thoughts together. A simple spiral notebook works well.

2. Consider which parts of the day you are dreading and which parts of the day you will enjoy. Take note of both, being as specific as you can be.

3. Reflect on and/or write about this question: If I did have the power to make my job better, the first thing I would change about it is...

At Work

While you are at work, try to complete the following assignments:

LEVEL 1:

*   Pay special attention to your "hot buttons" or what "throws you off" as you go through your day. Note the people, places, tasks, or things that have a strong negative impact on you.

*   Watch for anything that positively affects you. Note the people, places, tasks, or things that you most enjoy.

LEVEL **2:**

- If you experience conflict or disagreement, find a private moment as soon as possible. If necessary, find privacy in the bathroom! Tap your right forefinger on your left palm like you did during the three-sheet exercise and picture yourself physically stepping on to the third sheet of paper and "looking at" the conflict as an observer. Describe the situation to yourself this way to see if you get any new insights.

After Work

After spending the day observing your workplace, reflect on and/or write about the following topics.

1. When is it easiest to take a "third-person" perspective to see what is happening? When is it most difficult?

2. How might you help yourself to get into that perspective even under difficult conditions?

3. Who are the most difficult people you work with? Which coworkers upset, annoy, or generally bother you the most? Why?

4. What activities at work do you least enjoy?

5. Who are your favorite coworkers? What do you like about them?

6. What activities at work do you enjoy the most?

7. Imagine that your job is a person who wants things from you. Use the third-person perspective to look at the conflict between the two of you. What does each of you want and need? Why is there conflict?

chapter two

How People Act

Dr. Fisher's Story

As one of our authors can attest, a job can be painful no matter how good it sounds.

To many, the idea of a professor getting "tenure" seems almost magical; a guaranteed job for life, complete with the respect that comes with a doctorate. Among faculty members, it is considered a mark of success. Dr. Fisher had worked for more than 30 years to achieve this goal. To her friends and colleagues, she appeared to be doing what she wanted to do, achieving success, and getting paid for it.

Then she did the unheard-of. She quit.

What could possibly be wrong? Despite her otherwise optimistic nature, Dr. Fisher dreaded "dragging herself in" to work in the morning. She liked the teaching and the students, and she found the research interesting. Yet something about the environment was so unpleasant that it overshadowed all that there was to love. Worse, she had no words for the problem. She felt isolated from her colleagues, with no interaction or inspiration. At the same time, she felt there were no problems left for her to solve, nothing left toward which she could be driven. Was she imagining things? Was there something wrong with her?

One conversation exemplifies her entire struggle. The Department Chair was concerned about the amount of research money brought in by faculty. Dr. Fisher suggested that low morale might be contributing to the problem and recommended reinvigorating both strategy and commitment. She even offered to spearhead the effort. But instead of being enthused, the Chair seemed puzzled. "I counted the total amount of research funding the previous year and divided it by the total number of faculty," he said. "All of us need to perform better. We need to create specific funding targets and monitor individual performance. When results improve, morale will follow."

Dr. Fisher was sure this numerical approach would fail, taking away the interactive energy and excitement critical to the department's goals. Yet her Chair seemed so sure. She liked him and found him to be kind, fair, and intelligent. But she couldn't understand his position. Later, she found none of her colleagues would support her idea to hold a departmental "planning and morale" session either. Dr. Fisher felt ineffective and strangely alone.

When she quit, it surprised those around her. Wasn't tenure the "final goal"? Had she been chasing the wrong dream for so long? It seemed that way, but only on the surface. It wasn't that research didn't suit her, or that academia didn't suit her, or even that her particular position didn't suit her. It was just a misalignment between her behavioral approach and her environment, a simple and observable conflict. But neither Dr. Fisher nor her Chair could "see" this mismatch from the perspective of human behavior. If they had, things would have gone quite differently.

Secret 1: Observe Behavior

Not a New Idea

When you objectively observe others, there is always behavior to be noticed. You can be talking face-to-face, listening on the phone, or watching across a crowded room. The person you are observing can be in a meeting, on the golf course, at the mall, or relaxing by the pool. It doesn't matter! As long as he or she is awake, the person you are observing will exhibit behavior. And as long as you are paying attention to the right things, your understanding of the person's behavior will bring into focus useful information about what it means.

In fact, behavior has been a topic of study for literally thousands of years. Of all the secrets you will consider in this book, the first has been around the longest.[1] As a result, it provides practical information about your workplace that will help you to see things differently and to like your work. Your own behavior, how the behaviors of others affect you, and the behavior your job requires all can mean the difference between job satisfaction and job dread.

Behavior Defined

When we want to talk about what people do in the office, we refer to "workplace behavior." When someone else's child acts out, we label it "bad behavior." When prisoners exhibit "good behavior," we reward them. And when our own children are causing problems, we firmly instruct them to "behave!" "Behavior" is a strange term because it can mean many things.

For the purposes of your new perspective, we need a more specific definition of the term. Let's define that here:

Behavior is the way in which a person engages with his or her environment.

In other words, it's not *what* we do; it's *how* we do it.

Two Key Differences

Understanding behavior is easier than it might sound. You can wear glasses without knowing how to manufacture them, and you can observe behavior without becoming a certified psychologist. You just need to learn two simple differences.[2]

Differences in "Focus": Task Versus People

Imagine that you are waiting with a friend in a crowded restaurant. Someone points out a window to the street and says, "There was a serious accident on this corner a few weeks ago." Your friend looks out the window and says, "I wonder how many people were involved. I hope that nobody was seriously injured. I was in an accident once, and I think the worst part was the fear that seemed to set in after the whole thing was over."

Imagine now that a second friend joins you. You share the same news with your new companion. "It must have been quite serious," comes the reply. "There is still a lot of glass on the street, I count at least eight skid marks, and one of those poles has red paint on it and is bent over to the ground. I wonder how many cars were involved. I hope that the paramedics didn't have to be called. I was in an accident once, and none of the cars could be driven away, so a group of tow trucks had to come collect them."

When you observe someone in conversation or in action, you can ask yourself whether the person is focusing more on the "task" at hand or on the "people" involved. You can also think of this as the difference between paying more attention to "what" or paying more attention to "who."

A person who is more focused on the task (on "what")

- Talks about either the details of the task, or the broad plans or objectives related to it.

- Looks at, listens to, and pays attention to things such as schedules, goals, plans, and to-do lists.
- Is made happy or unhappy by *what* is accomplished or not accomplished. ("I'm proud that we got this done ahead of schedule," or "I'm concerned that we're missing critical details.").
- Might downplay the importance of team dynamics or "team health," so long as the job gets done ("I don't care if you don't like each other, as long as you get the work done!").
- Works alone to learn about new things.
- Thinks about new ideas or assignments in terms of goals, mechanics, details, or results.

On the other hand, a person who is more focused on the people (on "who")

- Talks about the skills and/or personalities of people involved with completing a task.
- Looks at, listens to, and pays attention to elements such as interaction between teammates, quality of teamwork, verbal skills, and relationships.
- Is made happy or unhappy by *who* is involved in an accomplishment or how people work together ("I'm glad to have the chance to work with Sue," "I'm proud that we worked together so well to achieve the goal," or "I'm concerned that there seems to be conflict brewing beneath the surface.").
- Might downplay the importance of short-term goals or schedules in favor of longer term relationships or "team health." ("I'm OK with missing this particular deadline because I think the team has begun to function more smoothly.")
- Learns about new things by discussing them with others.
- Thinks about new ideas or assignments in terms of the other people involved or the impact of the results on others.

Using this perspective, you can describe immediately the difference between your two friends' views of the recent accident. The first was clearly focused on the people—who was involved, how many, how they experienced it, and the like. The second was clearly focused on the task—what happened, what had to be done, the logistics of the cleanup, and related issues. Of course, it's not that one friend is smarter than the other; they are just differently focussed.

It is the same difference that Dr. Fisher experienced in speaking with her Department Chair about budget targets. She was focused on the people, while he was focused on the task. The difference in perspective, so clear when viewed as a behavioral difference, was confusing and disheartening without a context for understanding it.

This is the first of the two differences you must understand in order to observe behavior.

Differences in "Approach": Reflective Versus Assertive

Imagine that you are taking a course at a local university. You arrive early and are alone in the room when the instructor arrives. On entering, your new teacher looks around and appears concerned. You ask, "What's wrong?"

"It's unfortunate," comes the soft spoken and deliberate reply, "that the university struggles with the logistics of classroom setup. Although I requested that the furniture be arranged in table groups of ten people, it seems they have left everything in rows. Fortunately, I am here early enough to go over my materials and adjust my plan accordingly." With that, your future teacher takes a seat in the front of the room and begins paging through some notes.

Now imagine the same situation, but with a different instructor. This time, the reply to your question comes more loudly and more quickly: "Those so-and-so's in the Logistics Office have done it again! I told them three times I need seating in groups, and they've left everything in rows. Good thing I got here early! Come on, help me move the furniture." Before you know it you have been drafted into service!

These two imaginary instructors demonstrate a difference in approach. When you are observing someone, you can ask yourself if he or she approaches things in a way that is more "reflective" or more "assertive." One way to understand this difference is to think of "reflective" behavior as trying to *respond to* conditions and to think of "assertive" behavior as trying to *change* them. As we will see, this also has implications for the pace at which the individual will operate.

A person who is more "reflective"

- Takes extra time to consider multiple aspects of a situation before determining a course of action.
- Chooses an approach designed to work best within current boundaries.
- Is more likely to follow rules, instructions, or guidelines.

21

- Listens more than s/he speaks in order to build a more complete understanding of the situation. This manifests itself as being quiet, introverted, or even shy.
- Speaks slowly and thoughtfully, with long pauses, using carefully chosen words and subtle expressions.
- Would rather be seen as overly reserved than as inadvertently offensive.

By contrast, a person who is more "assertive"

- Makes an immediate determination of the most salient facts or points and quickly crafts a course of action based on it.
- Chooses a response that is likely to test, adjust, or completely change current boundaries.
- Is more likely to bend or break rules, instructions, or guidelines ("It's better to beg forgiveness than ask permission!").
- Speaks more than s/he listens in order to take charge of the situation. This manifests itself as being verbal, extroverted, or even domineering.
- Speaks quickly and pointedly, in an animated fashion, with very little silent time, using blunt or direct words.
- Would rather occasionally offend someone than give up the right to speak his/her mind.

Given these two choices, you can now articulate the difference between the two instructors using descriptive, neutral terms. The first instructor was reflective, soft-spoken and reserved, and adjusted to meet environmental constraints. By contrast, the second instructor was assertive: Decisions and actions happened more quickly; word choice was blunt. Everything in the environment, including what *you* were doing, was open to negotiation!

Once again, we do not label either approach as "better." You might find one instructor's approach to be preferable. You might even be offended by the other. But that response is a result of your own preferences and your own style.

From Two Questions to Four Styles

Now that you understand how to see differences in "focus" and "approach," you are ready to start using the behavioral model. To interpret behavior, simply observe a person carefully and try to answer two questions:

1. Is he or she more interested in the task or in the people doing it?

2. Is he or she more reflective or more assertive?

Even if you can only figure out the answer to one of the two questions when observing behavior, the answer can tell you quite a lot about a person and a situation. If you are able to answer both questions, you will find out even more.

Why? Each combination of answers is directly connected to a primary behavioral "style." And once you know which style is at play, you can draw conclusions about a host of factors, including what drives the peoples' behavior, what they need, what will cause stress, and how to best influence them. Thanks to voluminous research, this simple model can provide some of the most detailed insights available.

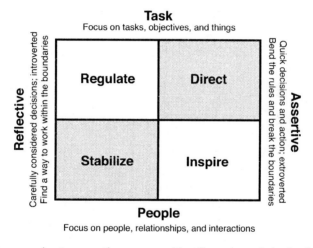

Figure 2-1   *By answering two questions, you can identify a primary behavioral style.*[3]

Figure 2-1 shows combinations of answers to the two questions. Each corner of the square represents one combination of answers and one behavioral "style." We label each one with a verb. The choice of a verb rather than a noun is not accidental; behavior is observable and active! We behave through verbs.

You have probably started considering which categories best fit your own behavior. You might also have started thinking about specific people you know. If so, you are on the right track. It's important to become familiar with all parts of the model, not just the ones that match your own behavior. We all struggle the most with behaviors most different from our own. Only by better understanding them can we can avoid the natural tendency to inappropriately label ours as "good" and others as "bad."

Behavioral Styles in Detail

After you have recognized a behavioral style, you can respond to it appropriately. Each type of behavior comes with a set of needs and goals, a strategy to deal with the environment, and a list of circumstances that will create stress.[4]

Task Focused + Assertive = Direct

Do you know someone who is always pushing forward, no matter what?

For behavior focused on *task* with an *assertive* approach, we use the verb "direct." This type of behavior in its purest form is about taking on a challenge and winning quickly! It is a quick, no-holds-barred attack on a problem or problematic situation. People who are using this behavioral style will be directive, assertive, and even aggressive. They will give instructions and not wait for feedback. Their need is to take charge of the situation and to solve the problem as soon as possible.

At their best, *people who exhibit directing behavior can overcome adversity and produce results in difficult situations. At their* worst, *or under pressure, those using this behavioral style might seem pushy, aggressive, dictatorial, and even mean!*

The combination of the task focus and the assertive approach means the person seeks results ahead of anything else. Speech and action happen quickly, with few pauses or breaks. Body language is assertive, and words are spoken firmly and directly. Often this behavioral style appears to others as "anger" as the person aggressively pursues goals despite any roadblocks. Statements such as, "I'm not going to put up with this," or "We shouldn't allow them to push us around," are driven by the need to prevail against obstacles, whether real or perceived. When the level of stress or frustration is low, the directing behavior appears as a person taking charge and taking responsibility for the result.

While many things can cause stress, anything that gets in the way of quick progress toward the goal or hinders the person's ability to direct the situation will be a strong frustration for someone using this style. Examples include schedule delays, disputes over who is in charge, and externally imposed restrictions and timelines. As stress increases, the seemingly angry behavior becomes more intense, and the person becomes more dictatorial and aggressive. This might manifest itself as a person asserting his/her position, giving orders to others, or becoming argumentative or even belligerent. Stubborn behavior is a definite possibility when directing behavior happens under stress.

Our best bet for communicating or influencing others is to try to match our approach to their behavioral needs. Rather than trying to fight it ("He or she shouldn't be that way."), we accept conditions as they are and then choose our response. Basically, we give the person as much of what they need as possible without sacrificing our own position.

For someone in the Direct quadrant, this means a focus on the results and an acknowledgement of the person's leadership role in achieving them. To the extent that it is possible, the person should be allowed to call the shots and move quickly toward a decision.

Communication strategies that work best with directing behavior are brief, task-focused, and decision-oriented.

The following statements are likely to be well-received:

- I don't want to waste your time, so let me get right to the point.
- You are driving the decision-making here, and I need your help.
- I have a problem that I don't know how to solve.
- What I'm proposing will help us get to solution more quickly.

On the other hand, statements such as these are likely to cause additional stress and therefore create conflict:

- You think you're in charge, but you're not.
- You can't do what you want to do (either it's not possible, or you're not allowed).
- We need to slow things down and be more careful.
- Let me show you the details behind the reasons why this won't work.

When dealing with someone behaving in the Direct quadrant, success depends on our ability to state the facts succinctly and keep the conversation results-oriented.

People Focused + Assertive = Inspire

Do you know a comedian, someone who is always the center of attention?

Behavior that focuses on *people* and takes an *assertive* approach is labeled with the verb "inspire." This type of behavior, in its purest form, is about actively interacting with others. It is a magnetic, charming communication strategy designed to engage others. People using this style will be outgoing and highly verbal. They will persevere in their attempts to make and maintain human connections. Because they are both assertive and people-focused, they will work quickly to find the interactions they seek. Their behavioral need is just that: to interact, to influence, and to be the object of attention from—and connection with—others.

At their best, people who exhibit inspiring behavior can be motivational, inspirational, engaging, and interesting. At their worst, or under pressure, those using this style might appear glib, superficial, self-centered, or even flaky.

The combination of people focus and the assertive approach means this person is going to take an active role in building human connections. Speech is quick and voice intonation is louder, as well as lively and varied. As stories are crafted and told, hand gestures and facial expressions are probably an important part of the delivery. The stories, while entertaining, might seem off-topic to those who are more task-focused.

Often this behavioral style is associated with an apparently high level of immediate trust; the person will share what seems like highly personal information quite quickly in an attempt to build rapport. Compliments flow freely, and statements such as "We have so much in common," or "I really think you'll enjoy hearing about this," come naturally through the dialog. A high level of creativity is often associated with this behavior and adds to the overall draw of the person's conversational style. If the stress level is low, inspiring behavior appears as a person doing an excellent job networking, creating connections, and influencing others to consider new ideas.

Again, stress can be caused by many factors. Here, stress comes especially from things that get in the way of interaction and interrelation. Personal criticism or doubt cast on the person's personality traits will add stress, as will isolation, confidentiality rules, or other constraints to conversation. In this case, the stressed person will seem to become less reliable as s/he focuses more on maintaining relationships than on getting anything done. Under higher levels of stress, the person will attempt to flee the situation as quickly as possible. If that doesn't work, he or she might take the conflict to a personal level. Insults and verbal attack are a possibility.

26

Again, our challenge when faced with this behavior is to remember that it is primarily a clue, instructing us as to how best to respond. Rather than fighting it, we accept it and then decide what to do about it. To best influence someone, we give the person what he or she needs.

In this case, the best course of action is to reinforce the person's social status and acknowledge the importance of the relationships they create and maintain. The person should be allowed to vent (after all, he or she is highly verbal), and then a solution should be found through conversation.

Communication strategies that work best with inspiring behavior are fast-paced and focus on reinforcing relationships and the status of the other person.

The following statements are likely to be well-received:

- Talking with you about this helps me to clarify my own thoughts.
- This wouldn't be possible without your ability to influence others to our way of thinking.
- Tell me your thoughts about this or similar experiences you've had.
- Who else do you know that I should talk to about this?

On the other hand, statements such as these are likely to cause additional stress and therefore create conflict:

- Hold your questions and comments until I am finished.
- You need to work on this alone and focus more on the details.
- Your input is not needed.
- Let's stop talking and get to work.

When dealing with someone behaving in the Inspire quadrant, the best chance at success is to give him or her space to create a personal relationship through verbal interaction.

People Focused + Reflective = Stabilize

Do you know someone who is always helpful and rarely seems upset?

Behavior focused on *people* that takes a *reflective* approach is labeled with the verb "stabilize." This type of behavior in pure form is geared toward creating a predictable, stable, and friendly environment. It is supportive in nature, with the person focusing on doing his/her part, building a predictable world, maintaining relationships, and not "making waves." People who are using this style will be friendly yet quiet, helpful, and supportive. Often they will yield to the needs or wants of others. Because they are reflective in their focus on people, they will relate to others without taking center stage. Their need is to support and sustain a stable situation through predictable relationships and minimal conflict.

At their best, people who exhibit stabilizing behavior can be loyal, compassionate, encouraging, and accommodating. At their worst, or under pressure, those using this style might appear territorial, defensive, petty, or even uncaring.

The combination of the people-centered focus with the reflective approach means that the person will take a more introverted, less emotionally intense approach to the important relationships around him or her. The person might on the surface seem detached or disinterested, but really it is just because he or she is staying calm and reflective. The overall pace of action is slower; conversations require more time, and there is more silence between statements. That's because speech is slower and words are more carefully considered. Hand gesturing and variation of voice intonation are minimal. Conversation stays on topic, with some time spent learning about others on a personal level. Those exhibiting this behavior are seen as very good listeners and supporters of a team or a cause. They are likely to finish what they start and to follow routines or systems closely without changing them. In situations where the stress level is low, the stabilizing behavior appears as a person following someone else's lead, doing their part to "stay the course," and slowly building relationships.

Quick or unplanned change, disruptions to the system, and unpredictable behavior will be major stressors here. Because the person's goal is to maintain stability and predictability, events or choices that impede this goal are likely to cause concern. When stress or instability increase, the person will appear to disengage, demonstrating a neutral or detached attitude. This lack of emotional display is often misread by others as agreement, but it is really the opposite. It's the first sign of distress, and the individual is attempting to stabilize things by turning within. As stress levels increase further, the person is likely to attempt to draw boundaries over what s/he can affect and what s/he can't. This often appears like territorialism, as the person might become adamant in claims about "what is mine."

As always, we can use our new perspective to understand this behavior and decide how we can best respond. In this case, the best chance of success is to allow time early in the conversation for rapport-building, listen to what the other person says, and allow him or her to find a way to engage that will not overwhelm the need for stability.

Communication strategies that work best with stabilizing behavior reduce the pressure for quick change, using a relaxed pace to establish stability through routine and relationship.

The following statements are likely to be well-received:

- I am enjoying getting to know you as we work together.

- Your steady contribution is valuable and continues to be necessary. Thank you!

- We will not make any changes without careful consideration of the impact to the team.

- It is important not to disrupt the routines of those doing the work.

On the other hand, statements such as these are likely to cause stress and therefore create conflict:

- Hurry up! There's no time to discuss or plan—the change is here.

- Processes don't matter; what matters is the result.

- Start doing things differently now; we will discuss the change later.

- It's not about personal relationships; it's about the work.

When dealing with someone behaving in the Stabilize quadrant, the best chance at success is to give him or her a chance to experience stability and regularity not only in the task itself, but also in the relationships surrounding it.

Task Focused + Reflective = Regulate

Do you know a person who believes that "the devil is in the details?"

Behavior focused on the *task* that takes a *reflective* approach is labeled with the verb "regulate." The purest form of this style focuses on following rules and doing things right. Those exhibiting it tend to be detail-oriented and analytical, checking and double-checking to make sure there are no mistakes. Because they are reflective about the task itself, their attention will be placed on ensuring that nothing is left to chance and that no detail is missed. Their behavioral need is to maintain compliance and control and to ensure that nothing about their work is below par or outside of guidelines.

At their best, those who exhibit regulating behavior can be quality-oriented, analytical, careful, and highly accurate. At their worst, or under stress, those using this style can appear fussy, overly analytical, and even cold and inhuman.

The combination of the focus on task with the reflective approach means that the person exhibiting the behavior will look carefully at every detail. He or she will act with caution to ensure that nothing is overlooked and everything is in order. Every decision is treated analytically, with "the facts" and "the data" being the most important considerations. Those exhibiting this behavior might be seen as fearful because they are so careful to consider every angle and every bit of information. The pace of action is slow, and attention is always on the task. Speech is slow and monotone, and words are carefully chosen to be correct and not to offend. Gesturing and eye contact are minimal. The conversation never strays from the task itself; personal interactions are treated as distractions.

In situations where stressors are minimized, regulating behavior appears as the person taking responsibility for quality by carefully double-checking plans and work results. In fact, those exhibiting this behavior are most apt to see their own personal value in terms of the quality of their work.

Emotionally-driven decisions, quick changes without time to calculate the consequences in advance, incorrect assertions, unpredictable human behavior, and sloppy detail work are all major stressors here. The goal is to maintain compliance. Those who push ahead, "damn the torpedoes," are seen as reckless and problematic. As stress increases, therefore, the need for control of details becomes more pronounced. The person might first appear fussy or "nit-picky," wanting more and more facts to back up each step. Under greater stress, "analysis paralysis" might also set in, and then no amount of data or information is enough to satisfy. In these situations, the person might appear to others to have shut down or to have gotten lost in the details.

As always, our new perspective helps us to analyze this behavior and use the information to decide how best to respond. In this case, our best bet is to reinforce the importance of correctness and compliance, keeping the topic of conversation on the task itself, rather than the people doing it.

Communication strategies that work best with regulating behavior focus on task, fact, and data and allow the other individual time to conduct his/her own analysis of the situation.

The following statements are likely to be well-received:

- Quality is the most important consideration.
- Decisions should be made based on facts and data.
- Take some time to review this information and decide for yourself.
- Mistakes are costly in many ways.

On the other hand, statements such as these are likely to cause stress and therefore create conflict:

- We are doing this even though we don't know the impact.
- You have made mistakes in the past.
- It doesn't matter that some data is missing or wrong.
- Rules were made to be broken.

When dealing with someone behaving in the Regulate quadrant, the best chance at success is to focus on the importance of quality and the impact of the details, and not attempt to use emotion or charm to influence the decision.

From Theory to Practice

You now know enough about the behavioral model to use your new perspective at work. The next chapter will help you do that.

chapter three

Watching the Action

Jamal's Story

Jamal's friends called him an "action verb." He was always driving toward a result, pushing the limits to achieve something new. Others saw him as a risk taker, but to him it was always about getting to a result. His biggest career successes had always come when he was directing the action and heading for a goal.

One year, Jamal took a job coordinating with community members, government officials, and private employees who were working together to create a new community center. To be successful, he had to keep everyone on task and get them to work together.

His biggest problem was Ryan, a state employee assigned to the project. Although it was Jamal's role to set the work plans, Ryan was the one who assigned them to others. If anything went wrong, Ryan was the one who had to get it corrected.

The first few interactions between Jamal and Ryan followed the same pattern. Jamal would outline the results he wanted and what work Ryan should assign. Ryan would nod silently and take notes. After the meeting, very little would happen. Jamal tried with each meeting to make the requirements clearer and to obtain clearer "consent" from Ryan. It didn't seem to help.

Fortunately, Jamal knew a little about human behavior. He knew that his own style was to direct—to call the shots and give instructions quickly. When he stopped to think about Ryan, he realized that Ryan's primary style was to stabilize. Ryan didn't like to make quick changes to what his employees were already doing. Jamal realized it was his own style of rapid-fire directions that caused Ryan to shut down.

At their next meeting, Jamal tried a new approach. He pointed out a major problem and asked Ryan to give it some thought. Then he left. A few days later he returned, told Ryan that the problem had become more serious, and asked if they could talk about it after Ryan had gathered his thoughts. Ryan suggested a meeting in a few more days. Jamal agreed, fighting his impulse to say, "No, let's meet NOW!"

During their meeting, Jamal spoke a lot less than he had before. He asked Ryan for his thoughts, made conversation about Ryan's ideas, and thanked Ryan for taking the time to think it over. Then he explained his own ideas about the situation, being careful not to give Ryan any specific instructions. By the end of the conversation, Ryan was recommending changes. He made commitments, and this time he kept them.

Asked about it later, Jamal admitted that it had been very difficult for him to adapt to Ryan's needs. "I wanted to jump up and down and say, 'Do it now!'" he said. "But I wasn't getting anywhere with that approach. This way, in a week it was fixed. The other way, I might have felt better during our meeting, but I'd still have had the same problem and been banging my head against the same wall two weeks later."

Behavior in Action

Conflict Between Styles

Donna and George managed a group of production workers. Their boss told them to find a way to increase their team's output by ten percent in the following six weeks. They could not agree on an approach. Donna wanted to make calculations determining how much faster everyone would have to work, write up the results, and distribute them to the team. George, on the other hand, thought they should hold a series of meetings with the team to discuss how the new goals might be achieved. Each was sure that the other's approach would fail.

Robert and Bill were negotiating on behalf of their company for a new janitorial services contract. After three rounds of negotiation, they had a final offer from their favorite provider that was within the acceptable range of their budget and needs. Robert wanted to study the offer carefully, and if all was in order, to accept. Bill disagreed. He thought there was still room for negotiation and wanted to immediately pressure the provider for a better price, without taking time to review the details of the offer. The two could not come to agreement.

Conflict can take many forms and have many roots. One of the easiest types of conflict to understand is behavioral conflict. Behavioral conflict can be observed between others or between ourselves and another.

Behavioral conflict often causes individuals to "dig in their heels" with respect to their behavioral needs. As both people focus more on what *they* need, they inadvertently focus less on what *the other* needs. This creates a vicious cycle, and the seriousness of the conflict often increases. One advantage of our new perspective is that it lets us understand and explain the *reasons* for a behavioral conflict. This allows us to adjust our own actions to better meet the needs of the other(s) involved.

The most basic behavioral conflicts usually involve a clash
between the answers to the two behavioral questions:
a difference in focus or a difference in approach.

If one person is highly task-focused, like Donna, and the other is highly people-focused, like George, the result is a conflict over what is important. The task-focused individual will see the people-focused person as being too soft or emotional, misinterpreting the people focus as lack of discipline. The people-focused person, meanwhile, will conclude that the task-focused individual is too uncaring and mechanical, misinterpreting the task focus as a lack of empathy about the human beings involved. This is why Donna and George could not agree.

If one person is highly reflective, like Robert, and the other is highly assertive, like Bill, the result is a conflict over how to approach things. The reflective person will consider the assertive one to be overbearing and pushy, while the assertive person will see the reflective one as weak or as being a pushover. This type of conflict is further complicated by conflicting paces, as the assertive person will want to act, work, and draw conclusions faster than the reflective person's comfort level allows. This was what happened with Robert and Bill.

Conflict can also happen between individual styles either because they are different (inspire versus regulate) or because they are similar (direct versus direct).

The goal is not to teach you to become a conflict mediator. But an understanding of human behavior will help you to understand the reasons you experience conflict with others and what you might do differently to improve the situation. Remember, your own actions are the only thing you control. Your behavioral perspective can give you a host of information about other people, but all you can do with that information is decide what, if anything, you want to do differently.

Myself, My Colleagues, My Job

Dr. Deborah Fisher (from Chapter 2, "How People Act") was being asked to adapt her behavioral style too far from its natural state for comfort. She experienced a high level of job dread.

Our new understanding of behavior allows us to "see" things at work that might have been invisible before. The relationship between our own behavior, the behavior of our coworkers, and the behaviors that our jobs require can be a major source of job satisfaction or job dread.

We can start by turning our attention to ourselves. It is useful to understand what our own preferred behavioral styles are and the extent to which we are allowed to exhibit those styles in the workplace.

The difference between the behaviors we prefer and the ones we use in the workplace is called our behavioral adaptation.[1] *If there is a big difference, it will cause dissatisfaction and dread.*

We can also consider which types of behavior are hardest for us to tolerate. As a general rule, the behaviors diagonally across from ours in Figure 2-1 will be the most challenging. For example, a woman exhibiting directing behavior will be highly stressed by a man exhibiting stabilizing behavior: She will be attempting to forge ahead and get to result, while he will want to hold back, plan changes carefully, and focus more on relationships and the impact to people. Dealing with the challenging behavior of others also causes us stress; in the absence of the behavioral model, the resulting job dread can increase dramatically!

By using the behavioral model to observe and characterize the behavior of an individual, we can more effectively adapt our approach to another person. Communication issues are a common cause of workplace stress; using the model to improve our own communication is an effective way to reduce our dissatisfaction and smooth the bumps in our jobs.

As we get more comfortable with our new perspective, we can use it to understand the behavior of teams and groups. Management teams, for example, have an overall behavioral "group style" based on the profiles of the individuals involved. Like individual behavioral style, this can be measured.[2] In the absence of measurement tools, it can also be observed. By watching the type, frequency, and results of the decisions made by a management team, you can answer the two questions of the behavioral model and determine what type of behavior *the team* is exhibiting. Knowing the "style of the team" can help you to better understand and predict the

36

team's actions and therefore help you better interact with the team. And better relations with management can definitely help you like your job more!

Using Your New Perspective

Observe without Judgment

It is important to remove any sense of "value" from the descriptive labels we use. That can be a challenge. Most likely, you feel a negative response to some of the verbs used here. The word "direct," for example, might for some of us call up images of pushy or overbearing people from our past. Others will respond in the opposite way, recalling respected leaders, athletes, and friends who held their ground against even the most challenging adversity.

Whatever our emotional response, it comes from our personal history, experience, and preferences. It does not come from the behavioral model or from the next person we observe. We must stay as objective and neutral as we can. That is the only way to truly change our perspective.

Neutrality is an easy point to grasp conceptually but a difficult one to put into practice. If you are struggling with this, consider some positive and negative contexts for each of the four basic behavioral styles. For example, assertive directing behavior would be advantageous when responding to an emergency but detrimental when negotiating for hostage release.

Similar scenarios can be drawn for the other three styles. By coming up with your own "pros and cons" for each style, you can help yourself stay more objective. That is time well spent because regardless of our own preferences, we must learn to observe objectively if we are to obtain new understanding.

Categorize Behavior, not People

There is a risk to using a simplified model in a complex world. Abraham Maslow said that "If the only tool you have is a hammer, you tend to see every problem as a nail." Over-simplification can lead not only to incorrect conclusions, but incorrect thinking.

While it is possible to measure someone's behavioral tendencies and adaptations in great detail, it requires more complex tools than the two basic questions in this chapter. These questions give a quick, practical understanding of *the behavior we see*, but they do not allow us to label the people doing the behaving.

37

After all, our internal behavioral "hard-wiring" is far more complex than a simple choice between four squares. In fact, one of the common abuses of behavioral models is to try to force-fit real people into artificial boxes by labeling them as "a this" or "a that." Some of the more popular models available allow for simple combinations of two of the boxes so that the total number jumps from 4 to 16 (4×4). But to say that there are only 16 types of people in the world is still unrealistic.

There is also a well-documented phenomenon of people using behaviors in the workplace that are different from their natural preferences. Sometimes our jobs force us to fake it! Imagine a shy and introverted person whose sales job requires him to make "cold calls." If you were to observe him at work, he would be behaving in an assertive manner. If you were to conclude that he is therefore an assertive person, you would be mistaken.

By focusing on behavior rather than the person doing it, we eliminate the problem of over-simplifying a complex human being and mistaking a temporary adaptation for a real preference. Instead, we focus on what is most important and practical: what that person is doing now. This helps us to choose our responses based on reality, rather than our perceptions of reality.

Use Your Experience; Don't Let It Use You

What about people we see often? Over time, for individuals we know well or observe frequently, we will build memory of how they "usually" behave. This does not mean that we have accurately measured their deepest tendencies, but it does help us to predict what they will do next. Here we must walk a fine line: On the one hand, our past experience is a valuable tool as we learn. On the other hand, we must be careful not to let our expectations, or what we "think" will happen, cloud our observations of what *actually* happens. If we do, we run the risk of developing an incorrect understanding of the situation and drawing the wrong conclusions. It is always best to separate our expectations from our observations.

Answer Only If You Can

Human behavior is complex. No model can fit reality all the time. Even if one could, no person could use it perfectly. Neither models nor people are infallible.

It will not always be possible to answer both of the behavioral questions. Often it will only be possible to answer one of them. Sometimes it will not be possible to answer either.

The two questions are designed such that when an answer is apparent, it is very apparent. If one of the two choices for a question is not a clear forerunner, all you can say is: "I don't know." This is not only OK—it is desirable.

It is better to have no answer than an incorrect answer because having no answer leads to more observation, while having an incorrect answer leads to incorrect conclusions.

In cases where you can answer one question and not the other, you have still gathered important information. By answering only one question, you have ruled out half of the possibilities within the model. Simply consider the remaining possibilities and use them as your guide to understanding and responding to the situation.

Your New Perspective, Revisited

The Easy-View Summary

You have now read about the basics of the behavioral model, the questions you must answer to identify behaviors, and the conclusions you can draw based on what you discover. Figure 3-1 contains the key to how the model works.

 Reminders:

1. Remember the *Tips for the Journey* (see Chapter 1, "The Trouble with Work").

2. Observe without judgment.

3. Categorize behavior, not people.

4. Use your experience; don't let it use you.

5. Answer only if you can.

Secret 1: The Perspective of Behavior

Interpreting what we do

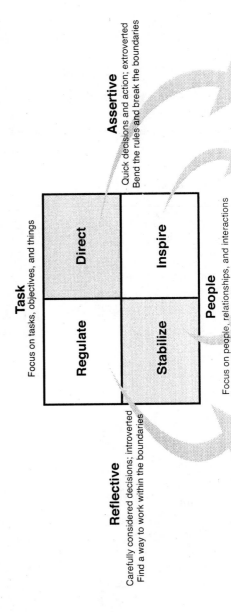

Task
Focus on tasks, objectives, and things

Regulate	Direct
Stabilize	Inspire

People
Focus on people, relationships, and interactions

Assertive
Quick decisions and action; extroverted
Bend the rules and break the boundaries

Reflective
Carefully considered decisions; introverted
Find a way to work within the boundaries

Behavior

	Regulate	Stabilize	Inspire	Direct
Focus	Task	People	People	Task
Approach	Reflective	Reflective	Assertive	Assertive
Behavioral Basics	Ensure quality through compliance with procedures	Maintain stability by supporting the team and following the process	Make, maintain, and influence through relationships	Solve problems by taking charge and prevailing against adverse conditions
Emotional Cue	Fear	Flat affect	Trust	Anger
Conversation	Factual, monotone, soft, few gestures/eye contact	Friendly, personal, soft, understated gestures	Expressive, quick, goes on tangents, loud	Forceful and direct, brief and targeted, loud
Potential Strength	Quality focus	Systematic and supportive	Motivational and inspirational	Quick solutions
Potential Weakness	Analysis paralysis	Territorial or greedy	Superficial and artificial	Dictatorial or bossy
Primary Need	Control details	Stable environment	Interaction and recognition	Direct operations
Stress Factors	Quick change, glossed-over details, unpredictability	Rapid, unplanned change or unpredictability	Criticism, impeded relationships, solitude	Challenged authority, impeded progress to goal
Under Stress	Picky, fussy, paralyzed by analysis	Withdrawn, territorial	Disorganized, flaky, personal attacks	Aggressive, belligerent, stubborn
Best Bet to Influence	Be slow and deliberate; focus on facts and data. Allow him/her time to do own research	Use systematic, relaxed, step-by-step approach. Avoid fast change (silence is not acceptance!)	Engage actively, allow for personal stories. Reinforce his/her value and your interest in it	Be brief and stay on task, respect his/her time. Let him/her make fast decisions, give authority

Figure 3–1 *Your new perspective: Behavior*

41

Homework: Before, During, and After

Before Work

Before taking your new perspective to work, respond to the following questions.

Consider the four styles of behavior: direct, inspire, stabilize, regulate:

1. How often do you exhibit each style at work? At home?
2. Which styles come naturally to you? (These are your own preferred behaviors.)
3. Which are more difficult for you to perform?
4. How much of your workday do you spend exhibiting the styles that you find more difficult? (Answer with an approximate percentage or a number of hours per day.)

Bring to mind one to three of your most difficult coworkers and consider the following for each one:

1. Which one or two of the four behavioral styles does the person most often exhibit?
2. How have you tended to respond to this person in the past? Has your response been similar to or different from what the behavioral model would recommend?
3. What are the positive attributes of the person's behavioral style?

At Work

Now it's time to get to work. Do your best to return to the third-person position to get the most out of your new perspective today. If you use the finger-tapping exercise to help anchor yourself (right forefinger on left palm), be sure to only use it when you are playing the role of a neutral, "fly on the wall" observer.

While you are at work, try to complete the following assignments:

LEVEL 1:

- Take notice of behavioral cues as you go about your day. When you talk to someone, ask yourself if they are being task-focused or people-focused and whether they are being assertive or reflective.

- Pay special attention to those people you find most difficult. Observe them in action and compare your observations to your guesses this morning about their preferred behavioral styles. *Let your observations guide you*; it is acceptable and desirable to adjust your assessment based on new observations.

LEVEL 2:

- Consider your own preferred behaviors. Notice when you are behaving in a way that comes naturally to you. Notice when you are forcing yourself to change to a behavior that you do not prefer. Take note of when this happens and of the reasons why you make the changes.

- Observe some of the other people around you—those who bother you and those you like. Do they exhibit the behaviors you prefer or the behaviors opposite yours? Take note of your observations.

EXTRA CREDIT/EXPERT:

- Choose a response to someone based on the behavior you are observing. It's not necessary to make this a major, defining moment, just a first try. Adjust your behavior *slightly* to better match theirs—perhaps increase or decrease your pace or focus your conversational style on meeting their primary behavioral need. Take note both of your experience and of the other person's response.

After Work

After spending the workday with your new perspective, reflect on and/or write about the following topics:

1. Which of the four styles of behavior (direct, inspire, stabilize, and regulate) did you notice most often?

43

2. Which did you notice least often?

3. Did you notice an overall behavioral "theme" to your workplace (a style that kept coming up, over and over, all day long)?

4. Which styles best describe your most difficult coworkers?

5. Which styles best describe you?

6. How does the behavioral model help you to understand conflict between you and those people?

7. Did you try any changed behaviors or actions? What was the result?

8. What would you do differently next time?

9. What else did you see, notice, or learn?

10. What were your two most important conclusions from this section?

EXTRA CREDIT ASSIGNMENT:

Choose a person with whom interaction is difficult. What is the issue? What primary behaviors are in play? Write about the other person's behavior, yours, and how they cause conflict. What can you do to make sure both of your behavioral needs are met?

Want More?

Want more information about observing, measuring, and learning from behavior? For more stories, exercises, and useful worksheets, visit www.likeworkagain.com/behavior.

chapter four

Why People Act

Edward Muzio's Story

A mismatch in motivation can change your whole life. For author Edward Muzio, it brought a ten year career to an end.

Ed started fresh out of college at a large company, helping to build the production facilities of the next generation. The schedule was aggressive, and there weren't enough people; he was perhaps given more responsibility than his experience level warranted. Luckily, he performed well. By the time the production facility was complete, he felt exhausted, educated, and exhilarated. Better yet, he felt like he fit perfectly with the company. He enjoyed work and looked forward to coming in. Every day, he saw himself achieving results that supported those around him.

Over the years, he worked in production, in development, and in strategy. He solved technical problems and organizational problems. He managed projects, programs, and people. At the same time, he trained and mentored newly hired employees to give them the same strong start that he had. In every job, if you asked him why he liked it, Ed would point to the results he could achieve and the people they helped. Eventually, he ended up running an initiative that provided resources and support to the whole company.

Then his department reorganized. His management decided to have him investigate his company's most complicated hiring needs and try to find outside programs to train people for those needs. They considered it to be a step up. Ed was appreciative. Unfortunately, his new work was abstract, providing only recommendations and general directions. He could not generate any specific results, and on a day-to-day basis he would provide little tangible support to other people. He was no longer able to describe his work to anyone, least of all himself, in terms of results or of helping others. Soon he ceased to enjoy the work and began looking for something else.

Ed didn't fail or get fired; he didn't suffer a breakdown or storm out on a moment's notice. He tried for many months to find a new position within his company. He couldn't articulate exactly what he needed, but he told his management that "this isn't it." But he wasn't able to describe his needs clearly. His superiors empathized but had many brighter fires to fight. After coming to the sad conclusion that there seemed to be no way out, Ed resigned.

He had been a strong performer, often evaluated above expectations. More importantly, Ed had seen himself as a lifelong employee. He had never considered resignation, and he would have toughed it out longer if there had been the promise of something better on the horizon. Meanwhile, as he was leaving, there was work going on all over the company that would have been a perfect fit for him. But neither Ed nor his management was able to understand the motivational mismatch that resulted from his role change. No solution was found, and both sides lost out.

Secret 2: Master Motivation

How Versus Why

Why did Ed leave a job that for years fit him perfectly? It had nothing to do with his behavior; he just no longer "felt motivated" to do the work. Behavior describes *how* an individual engages with his or her environment. Motivation, the second secret, lets us see *why* the individual decides to do anything in the first place. Both apply to every situation, but each gives a different perspective.

Motivation Defined

We hear a lot about "motivation." "I just don't feel motivated today." "How can I motivate that person?" These questions come up often at work. Like the word "behavior," motiviation is used in many different ways, some of which seem contradictory.[1] In this book, we use a very specific definition of the term.

> *Motivation is the unchangeable driving force behind a
> person's choice to act or refrain from action.*

Motivation is unchangeable. The deepest reasons for our actions are not negotiable; they are "hard-wired" within us. We don't even have the ability to change *our own* motivation on a moment's notice, much less someone else's. This means that the only way to "motivate" others is to align our requests with the drives they already have. When we ask someone to do what they already want to do, no "motivational techniques" are necessary.

Motivation works behind the scenes to drive action, often in a way that is not obvious. It is expressed in nouns, not verbs, because it describes reasons, not actions. Imagine yourself watching a train pass. Pure observation of the train will tell you how many cars there are, which way it is going, and how fast. This is like the train's "behavior." But observation will not show you why there are so many cars, why the train is going that speed, or where it is going. The train's "motivation" can only be determined through some sort of inquiry involving the question, "Why?"

We must constantly ask "Why?" to discover the motivating reasons behind what we see.

Motivation Versus Survival

"Motivation is easy," one manager said. "I either promise my employees something good or threaten them with something bad. Either way, it works."

This reward/punishment approach (called "the carrot and the stick") is often cited as a set of motivational "tools." But while these methods work to create a visible change in behavior over the short term, they are different from our strict definition of motivation.

Consider punishment. The avoidance of pain does inspire action, but it does not fit with our definition of "motivation." When survival is at risk, everyone will act to survive. This is an obvious instinct. When you put a gun to someone's head, you don't need a deep understanding of motivation to know that your orders will be followed. You also don't produce a permanent change in action. When you remove the gun, your "influence" goes away because you have not tapped into the true reasons for the other person's actions.

What about reward? If the "carrot" is something the person needs to survive (a meal, a paycheck, and so on), then the promise of the "reward" is really the same as the promise to withhold punishment, and the survival effect is the same. If, on the other hand, the reward is truly a reward, then we must ask *why* the recipient finds the prize rewarding. That is exactly what our new understanding of motivation will help us discover.

Basic reward and punishment are, at best, schoolmasters that help us discover what truly motivates ourselves or someone else. At worst, they are a poor substitute for real motivation and a heavy-handed way to inspire fear and resentment.

Building the Six Factors

Three Kinds of "Why"

When trying to understand motivation, we start by asking what a person cares most about. We answer that question in terms of the three basic components of every situation: tasks, people, and processes.

- **Tasks** are the things people do and all that is related to them (objectives, plans, to-do lists, and so on).
- **People** are the ones doing the tasks and all that is related to those people (relationships, conflicts, interaction, and so on).
- **Processes** are the guidelines, routines, and structures that people use to complete tasks (structures, guidelines, meetings, and so on).

Basically, tasks are accomplished by people following processes. This framework can also be thought of as *what* (is done), *who* (does it), and *how* (it is done).[2]

Invisible Versus Visible

The next question we ask is whether the person cares about things everyone can see or things only he or she can see. We call these the visible and the invisible.

- **Visible elements** are things that everyone can see.
- **Invisible elements** are things that only one person can see.

Imagine yourself waiting in line to purchase concert tickets. What you are thinking about and how many tickets you need are invisible—they are not apparent just by looking at you. On the other hand, the number of people ahead of you in line and the speed at which the line is moving are visible; others can see exactly what you are seeing by looking for themselves.

Six Motivating Factors

Answers to the two questions, what a person cares about and if it is visible or invisible, lead us to six possible areas of motivation, as seen in Figure 4-1.

In reading through this list, you might already have started to think about one or two that are most important to you. Most people are motivated most strongly by two of these factors. We define our most important factors as our passions.

	Invisible Seen best by me	**Visible** Seen by everyone
Task →	**Truth** Do I have the "right" answer?	**Results** What outcome does the task produce?
People →	**Power** Do I wield the most influence or control?	**Assistance** Who is supported or helped?
Process →	**Form** How do I experience the process?	**Structure** How is everyone required to proceed?

Figure 4-1 *Six possible combinations of the Task/People/Process decision with the Invisible/Visible decision*

A person's passions are the motivating factors that drive him or her most strongly.[3]

Passions are what drive us to act; they define our motivational needs. Understanding our own passions and learning to recognize the passions of others will help us to communicate more effectively, improve relationships, and reduce the pain we feel at work.

Connecting Questions to Motivation

Recognizing our own passions is easy. To recognize someone else's passions, we must answer only two questions (consider the *reasons for a person's actions* as you answer):

1. Is the reason based on tasks, people, or processes?
2. Is the reason based on something invisible (seen mostly by him/her) or visible (seen by everyone)?

By answering these two questions, you can determine the most likely motivational factor from Figure 4-1.

Answering the Two Questions

Discovering these two answers can be challenging because it requires you to ask questions that uncover the *reasons* for another person's actions. If you do so in an emotionally charged situation, the other person might feel attacked or put "on the spot" by your "why" questioning. You might not get the answers you need. Worse, you might damage your relationship.

Rather than asking "why" questions in difficult or charged situations, there are two approaches that are much more likely to give you a more accurate view. The first is simply a matter of observation over time. Instead of asking questions in the moment, wait and watch for the answer to your question to emerge. By listening carefully to what people say, how they explain or defend their positions, and what they ask for, you can often get strong clues as to the true answers to the questions.

Another option is to avoid the difficult topic altogether and engage in a personal conversation. Motivational passions don't change when people leave the office, so they show up outside of work as well. Basic conversational questions can give us a strong indication of another person's motivation without getting too personal, for example

- Preferences about vacations ("Why do you want to go there?")
- Reasons for favorite hobbies ("Why do you enjoy doing that?")
- Thoughts about home improvement projects ("Why did you decide to make that change?")

Asking any of these questions of someone in a casual conversation can yield a wealth of information about their motivation.

Six Factors in Detail

Beware! In exploring the six factors,[4] there is a natural temptation to read the sections that apply to you and gloss over the rest. But you cannot use the motivational model if you only understand part of it, and you have the most to learn about the factors that are most different from you. Instead of skimming, challenge yourself to read about each motivator carefully and try to think of someone you know who fits into each category.

Task + Visible = Results

Do you know someone who hates to waste time or money?

A result is what we see when a task is completed, so we say that results are the "visible" aspect of tasks. As a motivational factor, "results" is a practical focus on making sure that time, money, and effort are spent wisely.

Results-passionate people—those for whom results are a strong motivator— do not want to waste anything. They make decisions by thinking practically about benefit and cost or "bang for the buck." Purchases are justified in terms of the need for the item and the value for the price. These people are careful with other resources too. Time and effort, like money, are valuable in their eyes and must be "spent" wisely. Meetings and discussions must have a purpose and make progress. Tasks and projects should have a clear and useful goal defined before they begin.

At work, results-passionate individuals will make sure that money and time are invested wisely and that risks and benefits are understood before a decision is made. They will find ways to measure progress and to identify deviations or cost overruns as early as possible to keep the team on track.

Teams who lack a results-passionate influence might be at risk for wasted effort and expenditure or for "churning" on projects without clearly defined goals.

On the other hand, a results-passionate person might over-emphasize value calculations and understate the importance of that which is not measurable. Intangible benefits such as team member morale, customer satisfaction, or user "look and feel" might be viewed as being irrelevant because they are not measurable.

Teams that are heavily slanted in the results-passionate direction might make decisions that have intangible but real negative impact.

Away from work, the results-passionate person will still understand and express things in terms of benefit and cost. Vacations are chosen in terms of value for the money and taken at a time of year during which prices aren't too high. Hobbies will be selected for the opportunity to produce results or realize return. Self-managed investing is a popular choice. Home improvements or changes will be chosen to minimize cost, maximize usability, improve resale value, or perform some other practical purpose like correcting poor drainage.

A results-passionate person will feel stress when concrete results and return on investment are impossible to quantify or are treated as unimportant. Decisions made based on appearance, intuition, or subjective experience will cause the person to feel dissatisfaction and probably to distrust the deciders! Such a person will eventually lose interest in such situations and come to feel powerless and ineffective. At that point, the results-passionate person is likely to "check out" in favor of investing time and energy in situations that feel more productive.

The best chance at communicating with a results-passionate person is to focus on value and benefit. Emphasizing the measurable, practical impact of a proposal is the key. New equipment, for example, is bought to improve capacity or to reduce long-term cost; new strategies are adopted to produce more output for less effort. The clearer the picture of wise investment of resources, the more likely a results-passionate person is to support it.

Statements such as the following are likely to be well-received:

- The payoff if we do this is clear.
- The return on this investment is at least…
- The immediate investment is justified by the long-term return.
- This will be time well spent.
- This approach produces more benefit for the time and money than anything else we can do.

On the other hand, statements such as these are likely to decrease interest and satisfaction:

- It is not necessary to measure the return on investment for this.
- This feels like the right thing to do despite the cost.
- It's not possible to put a price tag on such an intangible benefit.
- Progress cannot be measured.

When interacting with a results-passionate person, the best bet is to think, speak, and act in terms of tangible, practical results.

Task + Invisible = Truth

Do you know someone who takes classes or reads obscure books just for fun?

While a result is what we *see* when we complete a task, "truth" is what we *think* about it. Was it done correctly? Only the person doing it knows for sure! Truth is the invisible, behind-the-scenes component of every task. As a motivational factor, "truth" is a focus on doing the right things right.

Truth-passionate people want to learn as much as possible—about everything! They wish to know all they can before making a decision, and they believe that knowledge is its own reward. Any kind of learning is seen as worthwhile. As decision-makers, truth-passionate people focus on finding the "right answer." An "incorrect" decision would be a major misstep, while discovery of a "new" truth would be an accomplishment of the highest order. As a result, truth-passionate people will gather as much information as possible, even if it seems unrelated to the project at hand. Lack of information is equal to lack of the ability to make a decision. They see meetings or discussions as avenues for exploration and discovery. Tasks and projects must be well-researched and based on data, fact, and precedent.

At work, the truth-passionate person will ensure that the right problems are worked on and that the solutions are correct and backed by research and precedent. He or she will be aware that everyone needs to develop new knowledge and will encourage coworkers to keep their education active and their skills sharp. As a result, this person might keep a team competitive over the long term.

Teams that lack a truth-passionate influence might lack discipline around fact-finding and individual skill development.

On the other hand, the truth-passionate person might over-emphasize the need for facts and research. Fast decisions, even those involving safety, might be ignored in favor of taking more time to find the right answer. On-time completion of important milestones might be sacrificed to the need for data. The person might be perceived as obsessive, myopic, or even scatterbrained as the quest for more knowledge leads to exploration of seemingly unrelated topics. If this happens, he or she might lose influence on the team.

Groups that are heavily slanted in the truth-passionate direction might spend too much time in the exploration and data-gathering phases of their work and not come to practical conclusions quickly enough.

53

Away from the job, the truth-passionate person will make choices based on "the facts." An ideal vacation starts with a well-researched hotel located near activities that provide the chance to "learn something new." Hobbies too are educational and reflect the desire to learn. If collecting is a hobby, for example, the truth-passionate collector will be able to describe each piece in terms of the facts and history about it. Home improvements are undertaken with careful study of "the best option." Expert sources are consulted regarding materials, brand names, and service providers, and research is completed before the first hammer is swung.

The truth-passionate person will experience stress if the discovery of "the right answer" is not necessary or not possible. Decisions made based on expediency, intuition, or appearances rather than factual information will cause dissatisfaction and might cause the person to distrust the decider. In cases where it is not possible to know the truth, the person will experience extreme discomfort. Over time, the truth-passionate person will come to feel disinterested or unmotivated by such situations and will begin to focus attention elsewhere, where he or she can be more inquisitive.

To communicate with the truth-passionate person, we must structure the conversation in terms of the current facts and the opportunity to learn more. New projects, for example, should be based on a clearly defined need and on the possibility of learning from the results. New equipment should be purchased only if it is considered best-in-class by expert sources or because it increases the company's capability to gather information over time.

Statements such as the following are likely to be well-received:

- There is clear precedent for this in the literature.
- There is a factual basis for this decision.
- We have gathered information about this over time and concluded…
- This will allow us to learn new things.
- Individual or group education will be enhanced.

On the other hand, statements such as these are likely to decrease interest and satisfaction:

- We don't have time to research before we decide.
- There is no right answer; whatever we do is fine.
- It's better to be first than to be right.
- Education is impractical.

When interacting with a truth-passionate person, the best bet is to think, speak, and act in terms of information and certainty.

People + Visible = Assistance

Do you know someone who always wants to help everyone else?

Assistance is the extent to which people are helped or hurt by any situation. It is the visible component of "people" because assistance is felt by everyone involved in a situation. As a motivational factor, "assistance" represents a focus on the human impact of decisions, programs, and actions, making sure they produce a positive benefit for others.

Assistance-passionate people are acutely aware of others' needs, and they want to help with their problems. They feel that we are defined by how we treat those less fortunate than ourselves. Serving as a mentor, developing a new course, or volunteering in a non-profit organization, for example, are all projects that have a strong component of assistance. The context or actions might vary, but the underlying intent is always the same. Meetings and discussions, therefore, should provide for the needs of all involved, including those not present. Similarly, a project or task should produce at least as much benefit to "the others" as it does to "us."

At work, the assistance-passionate person will ensure that decisions and projects are helpful and not harmful to people, serving in some sense as the conscience of the group. This person's value to the team comes from his or her ability to keep things human and make sure that the world is a better place as a result of the team's work. Ethical questions about impact to the larger population are never avoided.

---

*Groups who lack an assistance-passionate influence might be
at risk for becoming callous or disinterested in the
human implications of their decisions.*

On the other hand, the assistance-passionate person might inappropriately place the needs of others ahead of individual or team needs. He or she might struggle to take necessary actions if they have a negative human impact. Terminating a disruptive employee, for example, might be clearly necessary but avoided because of the perceived impact to the employee's family. This can lead to missed commitments, cost overruns, or other issues with the team's work. As a result, the assistance-passionate person might be seen as being too soft, "spineless," or "a bleeding heart" and lose influence within the group.

---

*Teams that are heavily slanted in the assistance-passionate direction
might sacrifice the needs of the company in favor of the
broader needs of "the people."*

Personal life choices of assistance-passionate people are also geared toward helping others. Vacation time is spent in service of those less fortunate, or else in support of the desires of others in the family or group. ("We went there because my son wanted to see it.") Hobbies are almost certain to include some sort of volunteer activity or community involvement. And home improvements are undertaken for the benefit of others who live in the home or for the comfort and convenience of visitors and guests.

Decisions that produce hardship for others will lead the assistance-passionate person to feel stress, especially if the hardship is not equally felt by the decision-makers themselves! Callousness toward others is a major cause of stress. Such a person will shy away from taking any action that will prevent other people from reaching their goals. If forced into such situations, the assistance-passionate person will feel "untrue" to himself or herself. In that case, the person is likely to disengage and seek other opportunities to be helpful.

To best relate to this person, we must focus on understanding and supporting the plights of other people. We should explain our proposals in terms of their benefits to a wider circle. Self-sacrifice must be carefully avoided, but at the same time there should never be an insinuation of insensitivity toward the needs of others. The clearer the picture we can paint of help being provided to others, the more likely the assistance-passionate person will be to support our ideas.

Statements such as the following are likely to be well-received:

- It is our responsibility to give back in some way.
- This will help others to accomplish their goals.
- What's most important is that our work produces human benefit.
- This will reduce conflict, pain, inconvenience, or suffering.
- Everyone's needs will be met.

On the other hand, statements such as these are likely to decrease interest and satisfaction:

- Their problems are theirs, not ours.
- We have to take care of ourselves first ("Look out for number 1!").

- Let's succeed first and worry about other people later.
- If you can get them to buy it, who cares if they need it?

When interacting with an assistance-passionate person, the best bet is to think, speak, and act in terms of impact to other people.

People + Invisible = Power

Do you know someone who can't bear the thought of somebody else in charge?

Power describes who in a group has the most influence. To have power is to sit in the driver's seat, regardless of formal rank or title, and control what happens. It is the invisible aspect of "people" because it happens behind the scenes. As a motivational factor, "power" is a desire to be the one in charge.

Power-passionate people stay focused on the question of who is driving and on making sure that the answer is always "Me!" They feel strongly that to allow someone else to direct their lives would be to give up their most important asset: individuality. Their strong sense of self-direction might also lead to a desire for power or authority over others.[5] Meetings and discussions are viewed as arenas to explore and assert individual power. Tasks and projects are undertaken to improve position, demonstrate clout, or otherwise influence the environment to accumulate more power or authority.

At work, the power-passionate person is an individual thinker and an empire builder. Emphasis is placed on the projects that get the most recognition, in order to build responsibility and visibility. Networking and alliance-building, especially with those further up the "food chain," are strengths. As a team member, this person will urge the team to take full advantage of both formal authority and informal relationships, helping the team to succeed. The power-passionate person is often adept at influencing or selling others on his or her agenda and can be a valuable "public voice" of recognition for the team.

Groups that lack a power-passionate influence might be at risk for "giving up too easily" when it comes to influencing, selling, or overcoming the perception (or reality) of insufficient authority.

On the other hand, the power-passionate person might not wish to join a team if he or she has little influence over its direction. The need to drive the agenda might run contrary to what the team needs! When the power-passionate person feels no control over the direction things are taking, he or she might struggle to take some control of the situation. As a result, the person might be perceived by the team as overly ambitious, power-hungry, or a "control freak" and lose influence within the group.

Teams that are heavily slanted in the power-passionate direction
might experience strife as members struggle for power.
Such teams might also abuse their authority.

Away from work, choices reflect the need to drive the agenda. Vacations are chosen "because I wanted to go there" or perhaps for the chance to build networks with other prominent people. Hobbies are geared toward alliance-building as well; if golf is in the picture, it is because of the arm-twisting and influential conversations that happen on the links. And home improvements connect with status or power as well; if the home is used for entertaining, then it is designed to be impressive in some way to communicate elevated stature.

To understand power as a motivational factor, we must realize that the question of who is in the driver's seat is different from the question of where the car is going. It doesn't matter whether the power-passionate person agrees with the *direction* things are taking. If he or she is not involved in *setting* that direction, then stress and lack of motivation will result. Any situation that does not allow this person to act under his or her own direction can cause dissatisfaction and disengagement. And if the person believes that someone else is trying to take over, a "counterattack" might be launched. The power-passionate person who is unable to gain the control he or she seeks is likely to feel like a "sell-out" and look for other avenues where more control is possible.

To connect with a power-passionate person, we must yield as much control and authority as possible, giving him or her a chance to voice opinions before decisions are made. Afterward, conversations should emphasize the person's influence. Special care must be taken not to ignite a contest of wills nor to create the perception that their power is being usurped by another. The more the person experiences a sense of control over the situation, the more he or she will be willing to engage with the topic at hand rather than struggle with the power structure behind it.

Statements such as the following are likely to be well-received:

- As a result of your influence, changes have been made.
- None of what we are suggesting removes your authority.

- You are the one who must decide how we proceed.
- This will allow you to be seen by and interact with other leaders.
- Success will create an opportunity to advance your position.

On the other hand, statements such as these are likely to decrease interest and satisfaction:

- You are not in charge here.
- The needs of the individual are less important than the needs of the group.
- Those decisions are best left to someone higher up the food chain.
- There's nothing you can do about that, it's just "how it goes."

When interacting with a power-passionate person, the best bet is to think, speak, and act in ways that reinforce that person's role as a major influence.

Process + Visible = Structure

Do you know someone who is heavily focused on telling "right from wrong?"

Structure describes the rules and regulations that govern any situation. It is the framework that people follow in the completion of tasks. We say that it is the "visible" aspect of process because rules and guidelines apply to everybody. As a motivational factor, "structure" is a desire to follow principles and rules in all activities.

Structure-passionate individuals have a clear vision of "how things should go," and they follow that vision carefully. They use one set of principles as a guide for all of their actions. This personal philosophy is how they decide right from wrong and make all of their decisions. And structure-passionate people will use the words "right" and "wrong" to describe the match between a new idea and their personal philosophy.

Structure-passionate people believe that there is a "right way" to do things, and they strive to define that "right way." They might define it in terms of current rules ("This is how the company wants us to do this."), in terms of personal history ("This is how I was taught to do this."), or in other ways. Regardless, they will expect themselves and others to follow their definition. Meetings and discussions are seen as opportunities to reinforce rules or processes. Tasks and projects are undertaken based on how well they mesh with broader structures and goals. In all things, structure-passionate people are careful to follow the rules and "do things right."

At work, the structure-passionate person will refer often to guidelines, regulations, and rules. As a team member, the structure-passionate person will frequently remind the team about both rules and philosophical considerations. This person might be the one who, at the outset of a new team activity, pushes the group to form a set of principles to govern the team's activities. This influence can be very positive, as the structure-passionate person can help the team to stay on course, both in terms of mission or objectives, and in terms of applicable regulatory controls.

> *Groups that lack a structure-passionate influence might be at risk for drifting away from their primary purpose over time and also for failing to comply with regulations or guidelines.*

On the other hand, the structure-passionate person might over-emphasize rules and regulations to the detriment of team output or relationship dynamics. Closely-held beliefs about how things "should be done" might be presented as if they are the final word, even if they are contrary to the opinions of teammates. The individual might come to be viewed as being a stickler or as being overly dogmatic about his or her own opinions. As a result, he or she might lose influence within a group.

> *Teams that are heavily slanted in the structure-passionate direction might risk frequent conflict regarding how things "should be" done. Too much attention to process and regulations might reduce the team's output.*

Away from work, the structure-passionate person makes choices that reflect his or her personal philosophy and the desire to follow a structure. Vacations are consistent with both; the annual family vacation might be to the same place at the same time each year. Hobbies too are connected in some way to the philosophy because it dictates how time should be spent. A structure-passionate person whose motto is "family first," for example, might use family time as both her vacation and her hobby. Home improvements are undertaken systematically in compliance with building codes and regulations.

The structure-passionate person might struggle in situations where regulations and guidelines do not apply. Problems that are novel or dynamic or activities that do not match the person's view of the "right way" to do things will create dissatisfaction or tension. The more the person is asked to act in ways that he perceives to be outside of his perception of rules or philosophy, the more stress he will experience. In such circumstances, a structure-passionate person will lose motivation and focus his attention elsewhere.

The best way to communicate with a structure-passionate person is to emphasize the regulations and systems of belief held by the individual. Consistency is a key word. Newer ideas and opinions should be expressed in terms of how they fit with previous ones, and emphasis should be placed on integration of new ideas into existing structures. Discussion of what has not changed, such as principles and philosophies, is useful. If the structure-passionate individual can frame a new idea or request in terms of the existing, well-understood backdrop, he or she will be less likely to object and more likely to engage.

Statements such as the following are likely to be well-received:

- This will bring us one step closer to what we have always wanted.
- This will integrate neatly with processes we already have.
- There is no change in philosophy or guiding principles, only adjustments to implementation to bring them more in line.
- This will not be disruptive.
- We will continue to comply with all internal and external requirements.

On the other hand, statements such as these are likely to decrease interest and satisfaction:

- There has been a change of philosophy and we need to get behind it.
- Rules don't matter, only results.
- We will implement first and work the bugs out later.
- Regardless of what you believe, you need to get on board.

When interacting with a structure-passionate person, the best bet is to think, speak, and act in ways that demonstrate the connection with the person's beliefs about how things "should be."

Process + Invisible = Form

Do you know someone whose physical environment must be "just so?"

Form defines how our experience impacts us. It is the invisible part of "process" because it describes the unique, individual impact that a situation has on us. As a motivational factor, "form" is a focus on that unique impact and a need to ensure that it is positive.

Form-passionate people pay attention to their personal experiences and try to make those experiences as positive as possible. Factors such as group harmony, process elegance, wall color, and furniture placement contribute to individual experience, so they are important to form-passionate people. Meetings and discussions are evaluated in terms of whether the experience is pleasant or grating. Tasks and projects are thought of in terms of how elegantly they are designed and whether or not they improve surroundings or process flow.

At work, the form-passionate person might seem like an anomaly.[6] His or her thought process might appear more intuitive and subjective than most, focusing on things such as balanced work flow or team harmony. While these concepts and discussions might seem vague at first, they often lead to very specific conclusions. As a team member, this person is quite adept at early identification of issues with team health and at gauging wider acceptance of the team's initiatives or decisions. At the same time, the form-passionate person's focus on process elegance can help a team to work in a more effective, balanced manner.

Groups that lack a form-passionate influence might be at risk for functioning clumsily and of not having their decisions accepted by a wider audience.

On the other hand, the form-passionate person might tend to conflict with teammates because of his or her different drive. As a rule, business is a results-oriented game; subjective conversations about "intuition" are unwelcome. Moreover, if the form-passionate person is experiencing disharmony, his or her attempts to describe the experience might be problematic. Statements such as, "This team is ugly right now," or "This process is too unbalanced," are likely to cause misunderstanding. The form-passionate person might come to be viewed as flighty or unprofessional and therefore might lose influence within the group and become isolated and disengaged.

Teams that are heavily slanted in the form-passionate direction might spend too much time building shared experience, focusing only on what is not measurable or predictable. They might therefore have difficulty producing practical results.

Away from work, the form-passionate person's eye for elegance and harmony will be apparent. Vacations are described in terms of "the experience of being there." Hobbies are based on design and expression; from drawing to gardening, anything that provides an opportunity to create something and then experience it is a possibility. Home improvements, too, are chosen to improve the feel of the room by changing color, arrangement, decoration, and so on. Function must never supersede form!

If the form-passionate person feels that a situation is undesirable or "ugly" in some way, he or she will experience stress and feel the need to make a change. Whether it is a drab gray room or a team with hidden conflict and vicious tendencies, if the form-passionate person experiences it as distasteful, he or she will wish to change the situation or leave it. If neither is possible, the person will become disinterested in and disconnected from the situation and will turn both attention and energy elsewhere.

The best way to engage with a form-passionate person is to treat his or her personal experience as a valid topic in its own right and seek to understand it completely. This person's intuitive insights need to be expressed. "What is your experience of the situation?" can be a powerful question. Care should be taken to avoid the suggestion that function should automatically overrule form. The more the person feels that form and experience are an important part of what is being considered, the more likely s/he is to engage with the topic at hand.

Statements such as the following are likely to be well-received:

- This is an elegant solution.
- Harmony and balance are important considerations.
- It is difficult to describe in words the experience we must consider.
- We are not done until the solution feels complete and whole.
- Everyone's perception of the situation is an important consideration.

On the other hand, statements such as these are likely to decrease interest and satisfaction:

- As long as it works, it doesn't matter what it looks like.
- We deal in facts and data, not in feelings or vague notions.
- Intuition is meaningless.
- It doesn't matter if we get along, only if we get it done.

When interacting with a form-passionate person, the best strategy is to look for ways to integrate their subjective experience with our own and with objective reality.

From Theory to Practice

You now know enough about the motivational model to use your new perspective at work. The next chapter will help you do that.

chapter five

Figuring Out Why

Ariel's Story

Ariel jumped off of the fast track. She used to work as an analyst, helping her company's software writers create useful applications by learning about the needs of their customers. She was so good at it that she was being groomed for management; her company wanted her to move into a position where she would oversee multiple projects instead of just working on one at a time.

"That's the last thing I wanted," Ariel recalls. "What I loved about my job was that I could learn so much about what customers really needed and then make sure that we produced it. At the end of a project I could see that we had gotten the answer right. Managers don't do that; they just push everything forward to make sure goals are met on time. They don't get to learn about the real needs."

In the motivational model, Ariel is truth-passionate. Luckily, she knew it! Instead of accepting the management position, she returned to school to study math and science. Along the way she had many doubts. Friends wondered why she would leave a good-paying job to be a starving student again. "They just didn't get that I like to learn," she says. "They couldn't see why I would walk away from that kind of career growth."

With her degree completed, she took a job with a research firm. Today, she investigates the causes for equipment failure using historical data and uses it to create more useful preventative maintenance procedures. She loves her new job and has no plans to leave.

"Here," she says, "my reward for doing things right is that I'm given more things to do right."

Motivation in Action

Motivational Conflict

Bella and Sally were members of a team working on a six-month project. During the first three months, external factors caused delays, and the project fell behind. Both women were committed to the project, but they had different ideas about how to proceed. Bella argued that by parallel-processing some approval sequences, they could recover time in the second half of the project and keep to the original schedule. Sally thought this was a terrible idea. She thought that the approvals were meant to be done in sequence because they built upon one another. It would be better to adjust the delivery date, she argued, than to take short-cuts on a proven process. The two could not come to agreement and brought their dispute to the team leader. Even after the leader made a final decision, the rift between Sally and Bella over this issue seemed to hang in the air during team meetings.

When conflict is caused by motivational differences, the reason for it is not always apparent. We must learn to recognize the difference between the *object* of a conflict, or what conflicting people say they are arguing about, and the *reason* for it, or what is actually causing the conflict.

When a conflict is caused by motivational factors, the reason for the conflict is different from the object of the conflict.

We rarely argue about our motivational factors directly. Usually, we argue about something more tangible. This can make the dispute impossible to resolve; it is difficult to solve one conflict while arguing about another!

Worse yet, in the absence of a common, useful vocabulary to define the real issue, we sometimes begin to craft our own. Recognizing that there is some deeper issue, arguers will say things such as, "What this is really about is your need to...!" Unfortunately, these statements are usually uttered in accusatory tones and rarely lead to anything other than more conflict.

We must develop the ability to see beyond the object of the conflict, to the real reason for it. This is the only way to truly address it. The ability to understand, articulate, and discuss the underlying reasons for conflict is a critical first step in coming to some kind of permanent resolution.

The most basic form of motivational conflict is a mismatch between passionate factors. Any of the six factors can conflict with each other. In the preceding example, Bella was more results-passionate, while Sally was more structure-passionate. It was not possible for the two of them to come to agreement over how to handle the project delays because they were not arguing over how to handle the project delays. They were arguing over their basic views of what was most important.

Could this have been resolved? Yes and no. It is highly unlikely that either of the two women would have changed their motivation. On the other hand, had they held a frank discussion about the real source of their disagreement, they would have had a much better chance of coming to some practical conclusion. Had each attempted to see and articulate the issue from the perspective of the other's motivational passion, then perhaps their end point would have been one that both of them could support, if not fully agree with. And they could have gone to their team leader with a joint recommendation, including pros and cons, rather than a squabble between two different positions. If nothing else, this would have been advantageous from the perspective of both women's careers.

Sometimes two people who are passionate about the same thing can also be in conflict. Two power-passionate individuals may struggle for control, for example, or two truth-passionate people may fight over "the right answer." And the factors can interact in more complex ways as well.

The intent here is not to train you to be a mediator, but to help you to recognize the potential reasons for motivation-based conflict. In doing so, it is important to maintain the viewpoint that no one factor is "better" than another. This can be one of our biggest challenges: to treat what we value as being "equal" with those elements that others value. If you are successful—if you are able to recognize the reasons for motivational conflict and you try not to value your own motivators over another's—then you will be able to use the information in this chapter to communicate more effectively with others and to experience less pain at work.

Myself, My Colleagues, My Job

When Edward Muzio's job stopped letting him help people and produce results, it stopped meeting his motivational needs: *results* and *assistance* (story in previous chapter). His satisfaction level dropped, and he resigned. Even though he couldn't describe what was happening, its impact was real.

The ability to describe and discuss what motivates us, our coworkers, and our job can help us like our work. If our work satisfies our strongest motivations, we will feel as though we are producing value in the world. If not, we might grow to dread our jobs.

Our motivational needs that are not met at work must be met elsewhere. If our jobs get in the way of those needs, we will experience dissatisfaction and pain.

Knowing our own "passions" also helps us to recognize our differences with others. If a person "rubs us the wrong way" or bothers us for reasons we can't articulate, there is a good chance that the underlying cause is a motivational mismatch. If the other person has little or no interest in a factor we are passionate about, it can increase that tension significantly. By asking specific, safe questions, we can learn volumes about the driving forces behind the tension. The new perspective we gain allows us to both think differently and respond differently.

Groups or teams of people have a motivational "profile" based on the tendencies of the individuals involved. Like the individual profile, this "group profile" can be measured.[1] It can also be observed. By paying attention to a team's decisions and outward communication over time, you can build an understanding of what motivational factors are driving it. Knowing this can help you to better interact with the team and also to predict its future actions.

Using Your New Perspective

Learn, Don't Judge

The things that motivate us are the things we value. As a result, it can be very difficult to observe others who are motivated differently without coming to negative conclusions about them. The observed, if sufficiently different from the observer, will often appear "wrong," "confused," or "bad."

When we have an initial negative feeling about someone, we must learn to treat it as a clue that his or her motivation may be different from our own.

We must take care to avoid judgment with our new perspective. The point is not to assess who is "wrong," but to understand everyone more thoroughly.

Philosophical considerations aside, judgment is detrimental from a practical perspective; it decreases the satisfaction level of the one doing the judging. If the goal is increased understanding and decreased work stress, then the best course of action is to learn without critiquing.

One Observation is not a Conclusion

Motivation is not easily visible. It will not "jump out at you" with every person you look at or show up as a clear answer to every question you ask. When it does appear by observation or conversation, the first factor that appears will not be the person's only strong motivation, and it may not be a passionate factor at all.

With motivational observation and questioning, the goal is to keep gathering information. Even as you begin to respond according to the information you have, keep questioning and investigating for more. Jumping to conclusions too soon can lead you to make statements and take actions that are mismatched with the person's true motivation and produce results that are worse than what you would have done naturally.

Describe Motivators, not People

There is an important difference between describing motivators and defining people. The point is to gain visibility into what motivates actions, not to permanently classify people into six boxes.[2] Effective communicators and leaders know how to classify and understand *situations* without resorting to putting labels on the *people*. You should refrain from trying to permanently label anyone.

Stay Honest

Knowing someone's passionate factors helps us understand how to frame communication and what components of a situation to emphasize or discuss to best get them to engage. Some find this to be a slippery slope that can lead to dishonesty in the name of influence.

But there is a real difference between emphasis and exaggeration; explaining is not the same thing as inventing. In dealing with a structure-passionate person, for example, it is one thing to talk about the structural elements of a new plan being proposed, but quite another to promise that there will be procedural compliance when, in fact, that won't be the case.

There are many reasons to stay honest, personal ethics and integrity being some of the strongest and most often mentioned. In terms of the goals of this book, there is an important practical reason as well: People who are lied to eventually figure it out. Many do so immediately, others not until false promises don't come true. Either way, the dishonest person loses credibility. Trust is lost, interaction becomes strained, and effectiveness suffers.[3]

The path to less work stress involves better, more productive, easier human interactions. Deception runs counter to that goal, creating tension, dissatisfaction, and distrust. It is far better to acknowledge someone's motivational needs and admit that they will not be met than to make false promises destined to disappoint.

The Easy-View Summary

You have now read about the basics of the motivational model, the questions you must ask to determine motivation, and the conclusions you can draw based on what you discover. Figure 5-1 contains the key to how they work.

Reminders:

1. Remember the *Tips for the Journey* (see Chapter 1, "The Trouble with Work").

2. Learn, don't judge.

3. One observation is not a conclusion.

4. Describe motivators, not people.

5. Stay honest.

Homework: Before, During, and After

Before Work

Before going to work, respond to the following questions:

Consider the six motivational factors: Results, Truth, Assistance, Power, Structure, and Form.

1. Which two most strongly motivate you?

    a. In what ways do you get the opportunity to experience these two while you are at work?

    b. In what ways do you give yourself the opportunity to experience them outside of work?

2. Which two do you find least motivating?

    a. Can you think of anyone who is motivated strongly by one of these?

    b. How does that impact your interaction with that person?

Bring to mind one to three of your most difficult coworkers and consider the following for each one:

1. Which one or two of the factors seem to most strongly motivate him or her?

    a. How sure are you about your guess? Why?

2. How do *your* strongest motivations compare to his or hers?

    a. How does this impact your interaction?

    b. How might you choose to interact differently, based on your new understanding of motivation?

Secret 2: The Perspective of Motivation

Understanding why we take action

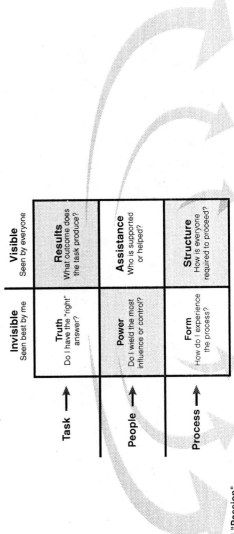

	Invisible Seen best by me	**Visible** Seen by everyone
Task →	**Truth** Do I have the "right" answer?	**Results** What outcome does the task produce?
People →	**Power** Do I wield the most influence or control?	**Assistance** Who is supported or helped?
Process →	**Form** How do I experience the process?	**Structure** How is everyone required to proceed?

Motivational "Passion"

	Truth	Power	Form	Structure	Assistance	Results
Fundamental Drive	To learn and discover what is true	To have in control of own agenda and destiny	To have a positive subjective experience of surroundings	To follow a consistent framework for all decisions	To help others	To investing resources wisely
Valuable Activity	Research, information exchange, education	Enhancing position, networking, self-assertion	Creation of harmony and balance	Following and reinforcing a valuable structure	Learning about and helping with the plights of others	Calculation of return-on-investment
Vacation	Investigated in advance, designed to promote learning	Demonstrate authority or build networks with others	Taken for the experience of being there	Consistent year-to-year	For the benefit of another person	Best value for the destination/time of year
Hobbies	Anything involving learning or history or facts	Alliance-building and business focused	Creative design and expression of it	Based upon structure and what is considered important	Service or community involvement	Stock market, real estate, other investments
Home Improvement	"The best way" discovered by careful research	Impressive and meaningful, done "how I want to do it"	Design, decoration, color to help "the feel of the room"	Systematic, in compliance with all building codes	To help someone else in the home	Maximum usability and resale value for minimum cost
Benefit to the Team	Education focus, research orientation, attention to doing the right things right	Advocates authority and position of the team; creates visibility	Gauges team health/team harmony and acceptance by others; elegant solutions	Consistency, adherence to both rules and philosophical guidelines	Tracks human impact of decisions and protects human interests	Results-focused and careful with money
Potential Weakness	Sacrifice of schedule, safety, or output to finding the "right" answer	Becoming too controlling or unable to "disagree and commit" with teammates	Overly subjective; loss of focus on objective requirements and results	Dogmatism about how things "should be" done	Sacrifice of self, team, or financial goals in favor of someone else's needs	Disinterested in intangible benefits, e.g. customer satisfaction
Stress Factors	Subjectivity, inability to know or learn the truth	Loss of control, others taking over	Objectivity, poor design, unpleasant situations	Unpredictability, ignoring rules and regulations	Lack of caring about others, activity which harms others	Intuition, inability to understand value or return
How to Engage	Speak in terms of facts and knowledge, avoid subjectivity or intuition	Focus on their influence and authority; avoid suggestions that they don't have a say	Understand and talk about their experience of harmony; avoid cold objectivity	Integrate new ideas with existing philosophy; avoid sudden changes in direction	Focus on the broad benefit to people; avoid minimizing the importance of stakeholders	Speak about results and outcomes; avoid "soft" or unmeasurable items

Figure 5-1   *Your new perspective: Motivation*

73

At Work

To discover motivation, you will need to both observe and converse with others. Take care to avoid emotional topics and highly personal questions! Stick to safe topics, such as preferences about vacation, hobbies, and home improvements.

Remember to use the third-person position, even when you are deeply involved in a situation. If you use the finger-tapping exercise from Chapter 1, "The Trouble with Work," ask yourself what the discussion or interaction would "look like" to someone watching the situation on TV.

You may need to ask multiple "why" questions to dig deeper into what is motivating another person. For example:

Question 1: What hobbies do you like?
Answer: I like to collect stamps

Question 2: Why do you like to collect stamps?
Answer: Because I find it relaxing and enjoyable.

Question 3: What is it about stamp collecting that makes it so relaxing?
Answer: Because I know what to expect; the collection is orderly, and I can keep it in order. Everything has a place and everything is in its place.

Likely Motivational Passion: Structure

Of course, it is important not to sound annoying or condescending by parroting "why, why, why" like a five-year-old. Just explore the answers as deeply as you can and see what information you can elicit.

While you are at work, try to complete the following assignments:

LEVEL 1:
- Without being too personal, casually ask questions about a coworker's vacation, hobby, or home improvement desires. As you are conversing, ask yourself these two questions:
  - Is he or she motivated by task, people, or process?

- Are his or her reasons for action based on considerations that are invisible (seen mostly by him/her) or visible to everyone?
- Pay special attention to those you find to be most difficult. Build your understanding of how they are motivated. *Let your observations guide you*; feel free to adjust your initial guesses based on new information.

LEVEL 2:

- Notice when you are meeting one of your motivational passions. Notice also when you are forcing yourself to do something that does not match your needs.
- Observe and talk to some of the other people around you—those who bother you and those you like. Do they seem to be driven by motivators you prefer, or are their motivators different from yours?

EXTRA CREDIT/EXPERT:

- Choose a response to someone based on their motivation. It's not necessary to make this a major, defining moment, just a first try. Adjust your interaction *slightly* to better match the other person's motivator and see what happens.

After Work

After the workday, reflect on and/or write about the following topics:

1. Which of the six motivational factors (Results, Truth, Assistance, Power, Structure, and Form) came up most often at work?
2. Which came up least often?
3. Did you notice an overall motivational "theme" to your workplace (a motivator that kept coming up, over and over, all day long)?
4. Which motivators best describe your most difficult coworkers?
5. Which motivators best describe you?
6. How do motivators contribute to the conflict between you and your coworkers?

7. Did you make any changes to your actions based on what you saw? What was the result?

8. What would you do differently next time?

9. What else did you see, notice, or learn?

10. What were your two most important conclusions from this section?

EXTRA CREDIT ASSIGNMENT:

Choose a person with whom interaction is difficult. What is the issue? What primary motivators are in play? Write about the other person's motivation, yours, and how they cause conflict. What can *you* do to make sure *both* of your motivational needs are met?

Want More?

Want more information about observing, measuring, and learning from motivation? For more stories, exercises, and useful worksheets, visit www.likeworkagain.com/motivation.

chapter six

What People Do

Erv Thomas' Story

Author Erv Thomas knows the importance of task balance firsthand. Not understanding it cost him a performance review and a setback in his career.

Erv was a designer who had never been afraid of an impossible puzzle. Over many years he had become known for his skill in solving complex problems. Eventually, he was offered a senior position. This excited him; it involved more responsibility, new challenges, and the chance to work on some of the most important products in his company. His career seemed to have switched into high gear.

For his first few years in the new group, he could feel the fast track. Erv won awards, got raises, and had a lot of fun! He had the freedom to explore new solutions to complex problems; as the cliché goes, he saw opportunity where others saw limitations. He would quickly design creative solutions to problems and then test them in the lab. Plus, he had a great relationship with the other members of his team. He even won an award for making the workplace a positive environment.

In the beginning of his third year the change began. Erv's group had become quite successful, and there was pressure from senior management for the group to create more structured, repeatable processes for their work. The company's leadership wanted to ensure that the group in which Erv worked could reproduce its performance in the future and teach other groups to have similar successes.

As a result, a strict control system was implemented. Erv could no longer select potential problems and work to fix them. He had to complete forms and documents about how and why he wanted to build prototypes and then get the necessary approvals. The same was true for the testing of his designs: He had to submit paperwork describing what he was doing in great detail in order to get laboratory authorization in advance.

At first, this was just an annoyance. Erv saw efficiency and value in having more discipline in the group. After all, he was able to continue his problem-solving work; it just took a little longer than it used to. What he didn't immediately notice was that he was losing the fun and energy he once felt about the job. And as the group's emphasis focused more and more on making the *routine* robust, the problem-solving freedom and creativity he had once enjoyed seemed to slip further and further away.

The problem wasn't just about enjoyment. The severity of the situation became clear at the end of the year during Erv's annual performance appraisal. He expected that he would again be ranked as a high performer. After all, the problems were still there, and he was still solving them, despite the more difficult working conditions. When he found out that he had been rated as a low performer, Erv's first reaction was, more than anything, bewilderment.

What happened? His management said that Erv still delivered excellent, innovative solutions, but he was doing so in a way that was not repeatable enough for the group's new standards. His solutions were difficult to reproduce and did not guarantee success. He was shocked and depressed by his first below-average performance appraisal in almost ten years. "But I'm not doing anything differently," he told his manager, "The rules of the game have changed!"

"That's the problem," replied his manager. The group no longer valued Erv's *solutions*; instead they wanted methodical *processes*. In other words, *the work itself had changed.* In the absence of a way to see and understand this change, Erv lost both job satisfaction and productivity, and his management innocently converted a strong performer into a weak one.

A perspective that allowed him to see how the work changed would have been extremely helpful. He and his management could have seen the change in focus and discussed it. They could have worked together on ways to allow him to keep using his strengths with the same group or to find a new position elsewhere within the company. Either way, both employee and management would have been better off.

Secret 3: Harmonize Tasks

The What

In the quest to not only reduce work stress, but also to actually love working again, you have to dig still deeper. It's not enough to consider *how* you do things and *why* you do them, but you must also learn to see the world in terms of *what it is that you're actually doing.* That is what the third perspective gives you.

The first secret we discussed allowed you to see the workplace (and the world) in terms of behavior, or *how* people engage with their surroundings. The second gave you a clear view of motivation, or *why* people choose to act. Both perspectives give you insight into how to interact with and influence those around you—and how the requirements of your job can be a good or bad match with your own tendencies. Task balance is the third major secret in this book.

Once again, it is time to set aside the perspectives you have used so far. In this chapter, you explore a perspective that is totally different from the others. So it's important that you do your best to "start fresh," to avoid confusing your newest perspective with the others you have tried.

Task Perks Defined

George Orwell once said that "To see what is in front of one's nose needs a constant struggle." His words definitely apply to this new perspective. On the surface, it seems inane to ask, "What am I doing?" This should be the one question we can all answer easily! Yet neither author Erv Thomas nor his management was able to discuss the answer to this question in enough detail to improve his circumstances. And Erv's situation is not unique. As you build your new perspective, it will become clear that there is more information in front of our noses than we realize and more hidden opportunity to reduce work stress as well.

How do we answer the mundane question, "What am I doing right now?" in a way that provides new information and useful insight? We begin by considering a very specific form of feedback,[1] one that comes to us from our own brain. Research has shown that whenever we complete something, we get a bit of internal, positive feedback from ourselves. In other words, as we finish up a task, we get in return a tiny congratulation from our brain to thank us for our hard work on whatever we just did.[2]

Whenever we complete a task, our brain rewards us with a small, internal "blip" of positive feedback.

This is not to say that each time you complete an e-mail, return a phone call, or sign a time card, you get a feeling of euphoria. But it is true that in each of those cases, you do get an invisible, miniature pat on the back from yourself as you hurry on to the next thing.[3]

Finding Positive Job Experiences

Imagine yourself in the following situation: Two years ago you were assigned the job of overseeing the construction of a new highway overpass. Your role was to select contractors, set a schedule, oversee the work, and make sure the project stayed on track. Today, exactly 24 months later, the project is complete. You have worked tirelessly and completed endless phone calls, meetings, contract reviews, and site visits. Now, you are standing out on the job site in the early morning, watching as workers remove the final traffic cones and allow the first cars to drive up onto the new overpass. You have succeeded. Imagine the feeling of success you experience. If you can, make a few notes about what this is like.

Now try a different scenario. Imagine yourself at work, looking over some paperwork that requires your signature. The papers are nothing complicated or involved, just routine forms that you are asked to sign every week. This particular stack has needed your attention for a few days, and you have finally gotten to them. Imagine that you are paging through them, one by one, signing each one at the bottom and moving it from the "unsigned" stack to the "signed" stack. Imagine the feeling of success that goes along with this process. If you can, make some notes about this and about how it differs from the first scenario.

In reality, the two situations provide very different types of task feedback. In the case of the overpass, you experience a long-awaited sense that you have *finally* completed a project. In the space of just a moment, you feel an intense sense of accomplishment that connects in your mind to a long period of sustained effort. It can be so intense that you may even feel something of a "let down" after it's over. Why? Because no matter how intense and enjoyable the sensation of final completion, it only happens once, and it will probably not be repeated anytime soon.

On the other hand, in the paperwork scenario things are more tranquil. With each completed signature, there is a tiny sense of achievement as you move it from one stack of papers to the other. As you go, you have the sense of the accumulation of achievements because the pile of "things to do" grows smaller, while the pile of "tasks completed" gets larger. The sensation with each signature is far less intense than it was with the overpass, but it repeats several times over the course of just a few minutes.

The two situations produce very different experiences because, as you will soon learn, they are very different types of tasks.

The Importance of Task Feedback

Did one of the two scenarios, the overpass or the paperwork, sound a lot better to you than the other? If so, it is because we all "play favorites" when it comes to different forms of task feedback. We tend to want more of some forms and less of others. Our preferred blend works behind the scenes to drive our level of satisfaction with the work we are doing.[4]

This is exactly the point of this new perspective. It helps you to recognize different kinds of task feedback and to identify which ones you are receiving. This allows you to adjust the blend you are receiving to bring it closer to your own personal preferences.

If you can do that, it's likely that you will lose some of your job dread and maybe increase your performance as well. It certainly would have helped Erv.

Types of Task

Task Type Defined

The overpass scenario and the paperwork scenario provide different forms of feedback because they are different types of tasks. To discuss how they differ, we must first define what we mean by "task type."

The kind of work required to complete a task determines the type of task it is.

This very simple definition is important to our understanding of task-based feedback because each type of task produces a different form of feedback.

The two factors that determine a task's type are how predictable it is and how urgently it must be completed. Any task can be characterized in terms of these two factors.[5]

Predictability

Predictability refers to whether the person doing the task knows what is required in advance. If we can "see the task coming," then we call it an *anticipated task*. For example, if every day when you arrive at your office, you check your voice mail and return the calls, then that activity is anticipated: You know you'll be doing it tomorrow and next week because you always do it. On the other hand, tasks that are less anticipated and more surprising are called *unforeseen tasks*. If your office has been in the same location for five years, and your employer tells you that you need to plan to move your desk to a new office, that task would be classified as unforeseen because it is new and novel.

Whether a task is anticipated or unforeseen is determined by whether the person doing it would have *expected* to be doing it. The decision does not have anything to do with whether the person is likely to succeed, whether he or she knows how to do it, or whether the final outcome is known or unknown. Those things, while important in other ways, don't matter at all when determining task type.

Urgency

The second factor in determining task type is urgency. The urgency of a task relates to how soon it must be completed. If a task must be completed as soon as possible, we label it as *immediate*. For example, returning calls from messages on voice mail is something that is relatively immediate; it would not be appropriate (in most situations) to wait a few months before returning someone's call! In contrast, tasks that can be put off for longer periods of time are called *deliberate*. These are the tasks that are not immediately pressing but can be planned and put off into the future. Preventative maintenance on equipment often falls into this category; it is something that needs to be done eventually but is not something that must be completed in a hurry.

Determining Task Type

In reality, both predictability and urgency are more like continuous scales than discrete decisions. Some tasks are more urgent than others, and some are more foreseeable than others.

For our purposes, we simply decide as best we can between the endpoints of the scales, answering the two basic questions:

1. Is the task anticipated or unforeseen?
2. Is the task immediate or deliberate?

The Task Type Matrix

As usual, your new perspective involves a simple matrix. The matrix defines a task's type based on the answers to the two questions.

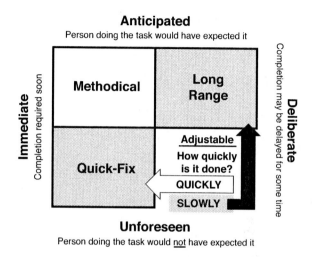

Figure 6-1   *Answers to two questions help us determine task type.*[6]

Each task type in Figure 6-1 provides a different form of feedback or reward when it is completed. Remember, we all have our own "special blend" of feedback that we want to get. The only way to get it is to make sure we are working on the right kinds of tasks!

Task Types in Detail

Anticipated + Deliberate = Long Range

We begin with the task type that is anticipated and deliberate. The Long Range task has its name because not only are we expecting it for a long period of time, but we are also able to work on it during the whole time we expect it. Building a highway overpass, planning a new software release, or working on a team to revamp an outdated business process are examples of Long Range tasks. These tasks are typically projects in which the end state is determined in advance ("Build the overpass."), but some of the details are determined as time goes on ("Which contractor should we use for the traffic lights?").

Imagine again that you have successfully overseen the construction of the highway overpass. This time, as you are standing there in the early morning reflecting on your success, picture yourself thinking back to the first day that you were given the assignment. Remember (in your imagination) how you were given a fixed budget of 2 million dollars to complete the overpass. You were given some specific requirements (number of lanes, lane width, and so on), but you also had a lot of discretion in how it would be accomplished and what the final result would look like. As you think back to that first day, what was it that you did that made you successful? What did you do in the following days and weeks to make sure that everything went smoothly?

Your answer probably includes educating yourself about what was required, writing a schedule or plan of some kind, and contacting others who could provide advice, services, and supplies.

These, in fact, are the typical elements of a Long Range task[7]:

- **Goals**—When the result is off in the distant future, it is important that it is defined as clearly as possible so that there is no misunderstanding later.
- **Planning**—It is necessary to make a plan so that the work can be accomplished in manageable and understandable chunks.
- **Resources**—It is essential to make good use of the equipment, labor, expertise, and other resources needed to reach the goal.

If you adequately address these three areas and you also manage to deal with all of the other things that come up along the way, you can successfully complete even the most complex Long Range task. And when you do, whatever other reward you receive, you also get the corresponding type of task feedback that comes from your own brain!

Feedback from Long Range tasks is the most infrequent and intense.

The feeling of satisfaction you have after completing a long-term project sometimes comes only after months or even years of effort. As a result, it is an intense, strong feeling that "I finally did it!" When it is over, it may not return again for a number of months or years.

Those who prefer this forceful and infrequent type of feedback will naturally gravitate toward Long Range tasks. They will come to love "the rush" that goes with finally completing a difficult project. In the workplace, they will want to work on and/or initiate projects that persist over time to create a change or improvement. At home, they will undertake more complicated household tasks and ventures that have a longer time horizon for completion. Checking e-mail at the office or cleaning the bathroom at home will not provide the desired experience. But revamping the office e-mail system or remodeling the master bathroom at home will!

If individuals who thrive in Long Range work do not experience enough of this type of feedback, they are likely to feel dissatisfied or "antsy." If they are unable to find different tasks that more closely match their needs, they may seek out ways to convert their current workload into Long Range tasks. Depending on how these conversions are handled, they may create issues or cause inappropriate focus.

In the next chapter we discuss conversions between task types. For now, the point to remember is that if people have a need for the intense, infrequent feedback that comes from Long Range tasks, they will try to fill that need and be unhappy if they are unable to do so.

Anticipated + Immediate = Methodical

Like the Long Range task, the Methodical task is also anticipated. The difference is that the Methodical task is immediate. Although we "see it coming" for some time, we are unable to work on the Methodical task until just before the result is required. Responding to voice- or e-mail, signing weekly time sheets, and entering daily data into a tracking system are all examples of Methodical tasks. These are things that we do on such a regular basis that their absence would raise more attention than their presence. They come up routinely. When they do, they require our immediate attention.

Let's return to the second of the situations that you imagined earlier in the chapter. Picture yourself again paging through routine forms, signing them one at a time and moving them from the "incomplete" stack to the "complete" stack. As you go, one stack shrinks, and the other one grows until after awhile there is nothing left to sign. Now imagine that this signing process is critically important to the success of your company and that you have been recognized as one of the best performers in this area. Your management has asked you to share your tips with others who have similar responsibilities. What will you tell them? How do you go about making sure that you complete your processing reliably?

Your answer probably includes some sort of organizational scheme, perhaps an inbox and outbox, to make sure the forms don't get missed or misplaced. You may also have chosen a time each week or each day to take care of the inbox contents. And you have probably built good discipline or habits over the (imaginary) years to make sure that you do what is needed.

These, in fact, are the typical elements of a Methodical task.

- **System**—When something comes up regularly, it is useful to handle it in a systematic fashion so that it becomes a regular part of the workday, rather than a disruption.

- **Schedule**—When fast completion is needed on a predictable basis, then it is advisable to build regular work time into one's daily or weekly schedule.

- **Habit**—Good discipline is essential to the reliable completion of predictable tasks.

If you successfully incorporate these three elements into the completion of your routine tasks and you are able to deal with all of the related issues that come up, then you will become a dependable completer of Methodical tasks. You will also experience the internal feedback that comes from the completion of that type of task.

Feedback from Methodical tasks is the most frequent and mild.

This feedback is the exact opposite of the feedback from Long Range tasks. A small feeling of satisfaction accompanies each item as it is "checked off" the list or moved into the "complete" stack. Although each individual feeling has very little intensity, the feeling can be repeated many times in even just a few minutes as it is produced again and again, every step of the way.

Those who prefer this type of mild, repetitive feedback will gravitate toward Methodical tasks. They will enjoy the feeling of satisfaction that comes with each check-mark on the to-do list. In the workplace, they will work on routine tasks and complete them in a predictable way. For example, they may have a fixed time each day at which they return calls or check e-mail. At home, they will also use checklists and processes to execute repetitive activities. The bathroom is not only cleaned each week, but it is cleaned at the same time each week, and the steps are completed in the same order.

If they do not have enough opportunity to experience this type of feedback, these people will probably feel dissatisfied or perhaps "stressed" by the inability to complete regular tasks on a regular basis. Over time, they may look for ways to convert other task types into routine tasks. This may cause issues, as we discuss in the next chapter.

Those who are not getting enough of the mild, regular feedback that comes with Methodical tasks will try to fill their need, and they will be unhappy if they are unable to do so.

Unforseen + Immediate = Quick-Fix

The Quick-Fix task can be the most startling of the task types. Because it is unforeseen, there is no way to expect or predict what it will require until it has arrived. Because it is immediate, it must be worked on or solved as rapidly as possible. Repairing a crashed computer, responding to a customer complaint, and correcting a newly discovered error in a software program are all examples of Quick-Fix tasks. By their nature, these tasks usually represent a high-priority problem of some kind.

Imagine yourself at work one evening, using one of a few shared computers to process some items that are required for an important meeting in the morning. As you are about to start working, the software you were going to use closes down, and an error message comes up on the screen. You know that at this hour you will not be able to reach any computer support people, but you really need to get this work done tonight. Under the computer you notice the packaging from the software, including manuals and a CDROM. So you decide to try to fix the problem yourself. You struggle at first, but then you have a breakthrough. You smile to yourself, and soon you are back on track doing your work as planned.

Imagine now that it is the next day, and all of your work was submitted on time. You mention to one of your coworkers that software problems almost prevented you from being successful last night. He seems interested and asks how you went about getting your work done. What do you say?

Your answer probably includes some sort of statement of the problem: "I knew if I couldn't get the software working, then the material wouldn't be ready for the meeting." You probably also make mention of the reason for the problem, if you discovered it: "Once I figured out why it wouldn't start up, I knew what to do." And even if you don't know exactly why it worked, you will most likely make mention of the solution or whatever you did that made the problem go away.

These, in fact, are the typical elements of the Quick-Fix task:[8]

- **Problem**—The driving force behind a Quick-Fix task is usually some sort of urgent problem. It is important to understand the problem before trying to solve it because different problem definitions lead to different solutions.

- **Reason**—The real reason for the problem is sometimes called the "root cause." This is what must be addressed in order to solve the problem. Ideally this identification happens consciously, but sometimes the reason is addressed accidentally through trial and error.
- **Solution**—Whatever addresses the reason and removes the problem is the solution.

Notice the close link between Problem, Reason, and Solution. If the problem is that "this computer doesn't work," then the reason must be related to the computer itself, as is the solution (for example, "uninstall and reinstall the software"). On the other hand, if the problem is "I can't get my work done," and the reason is "this computer doesn't work," then the solution relates to *getting the work done*, so it can be quite different (for example, "move to a different computer"). Either of these may have been the breakthrough you had, depending upon how you defined the problem in your imaginary scenario.

The important thing is that all elements are present and that they relate in a logical fashion. If you successfully discover and address these three aspects of your Quick-Fix task, and you also are able to deal with all of the related issues that come up, then you will be likely to resolve whatever issue you are working on. When you do, you will experience the internal sensation of feedback associated with Quick-Fix tasks.

The feedback that comes from Quick-Fix tasks is essentially "in between" the other two types of feedback.

This feedback is not as infrequent nor as intense as the feedback from Long Range tasks. Fixing the computer is not as exciting as completing the overpass, and it happens more often! On the other hand, it is neither as frequent nor as mild as the feedback from Methodical tasks. Fixing the computer *is* more exciting than signing the paperwork, and we all hope that it happens less frequently.

Those who prefer this middle ground of feedback will gravitate toward Quick-Fix tasks. These people enjoy the rush of finally coming to solution on a problem but wouldn't want to wait months or years for the next one. They most likely enjoy "the hunt," tracking down the reason for a problem and then figuring out how to solve it. Once it is solved, the problem is put behind them, and they can move on to the next one. At home, they will also look for problems to solve. They might not want to remodel the bathroom, and they might not have a consistent method for cleaning it, but if there is a leaky pipe, they will be the first one on the scene!

People who don't receive as much Quick-Fix feedback as they need will feel frustrated or "held back" by the lack of opportunity to solve problems. Over time, if they are unable to find opportunities to work in this way, they may seek ways to convert other task types into Quick-Fix tasks. While conversions between task types are discussed in the next chapter, it is worth noting here that converting other task types to Quick-Fix tasks is especially risky because it often involves the installation of false urgency!

In any case, those who are not getting their fill of the feedback that comes from Quick-Fix tasks are likely to feel dissatisfaction as they struggle to fill their need.

Unforseen + Deliberate = Adjustable

The Adjustable task is both unforeseen and deliberate. Although it comes up with little warning, once it arises, there is a long period of time in which to work on it. As a result, it can be treated like a Long Range task. This is usually what happens, especially when a person has only a small number of Adjustable tasks to address.

Sometimes a deadline may be set sooner for the Adjustable task. In that case, the Adjustable task is treated like a Quick-Fix task. This usually happens when the person doing the task has a long list of Adjustable tasks to address.

Adjustable tasks do not have their own form of feedback or their own requirements.

The feedback that comes from adjustable tasks depends upon what type of tasks they become.

From Theory to Practice

You now know enough about task balance to use your new perspective at work. Our next chapter will help you do that.

chapter seven

Do What You Like

Conrad's Story

Conrad was destined for great things. He just needed to switch gears first. Luckily, his friend knew it.

He had been excited to get his job at the water treatment plant. He found the work interesting and saw the chance to build a career. Most of Conrad's duties involved the routine; he kept systems running and monitored output. He also did a bit of project work, serving as a member of a team that was working on improvements to the line. After six or eight months, his managers thought his work was adequate, and he had settled in to a job he referred to as "OK."

Conrad had become friends with one of his coworkers, Sylvia. Over time, Sylvia noticed something that even Conrad missed. Although his work on the routine part of his job was just adequate, Conrad's level of enthusiasm, engagement, and performance on the project team was much higher. He brought new ideas to the team, never missed a commitment to them, and often volunteered to take on extra pieces of the team's work.

Sylvia pointed this out to Conrad and suggested that he apply for a transfer. There was a group within the plant, she explained, that spent most of its time on projects to improve the plant. Since he seemed to like the project-type work, perhaps he would like that better?

Conrad was hesitant. A transfer had not been in his plans, and he knew that things were all right where he was. "Sure," he said, "I don't 'love' this job, but I don't hate it either. Plus, I'm doing OK. I'm not sure I should risk that." But Sylvia was persistent. She kept bringing him information about the other group and even introduced him to their manager. He had to admit, it did sound like fun.

Conrad transferred. Within a year, he was a star performer and had won a major award. "I'm amazed," he told Sylvia, "at how easy it is to be good at this job. I love it!"

Task Balance in Action

Task Type Conflict

Our understanding of task balance helps us to focus on our tasks themselves. As a result, we are able to see a type of conflict that is not terribly obvious to the "naked eye": conflict between a person and the thing s/he is doing.

If our actual blend of task types is too far from our ideal blend, we experience Task Type Conflict.[1]

Task Type Conflict comes from the overall blend of tasks, not any one individual task itself. If, for example, you hate to sweep because you were forced to sweep daily as a child, then you are going to avoid sweeping. This is not an example of Task Type Conflict because it doesn't take the task balance model to figure out that you are going to experience "dissatisfaction" with that particular task.

Task Type Conflict is not about whether you love or hate the specific thing you are doing at the moment. It is about whether that "thing" represents too much of a certain type of task for you, within the context of the whole day or week. You might not mind checking your e-mail or signing paperwork as individual activities, but if you just finished spending several hours doing some other Methodical tasks, then you might find those activities very dissatisfying *in the moment*. If, on the other hand, you just spent a whole day focused exclusively on some Long Range project planning, you might welcome the chance to work on some Methodical tasks.

As a rule of thumb, when you find yourself aggravated, frustrated, or restless because of a task that you have done before without these negative feelings, the central issue is probably a Task Type Conflict. This is the power of the task balance perspective: it can help you to understand why this is happening and to adjust accordingly.

Myself, My Colleagues, My Job

Like you, those around you might also be experiencing Task Type Conflict with their work. If they lack an understanding of task balance, they probably experience it as general unhappiness, rather than as a specific and fixable issue. There are three reasons why it might be useful for you to recognize when others are experiencing Task Type Conflict.

First, Task Type Conflict causes stress. That stress often manifests itself in other ways. So you might recognize stress using one of the other perspectives, but it might take the task balance perspective to understand the reason for it. Recall the story of Erv Thomas' loss in productivity when the work of his group changed (Chapter 6, "What People Do"). By the time his management was communicating his poor performance results, he was obviously under considerable tension and no longer enjoying his job. He probably would have exhibited signs of stress, perhaps acting more irritable and tired. A caring manager might have recommended that he "get some rest" or "take a vacation." These might have been solutions to the obvious, visible issues, but they would have done nothing to address the real cause of his stress.

Second, Task Type Conflict hurts performance. As we get further and further from our preferred blend of tasks, we begin to make inappropriate conversions between task types. Robbed of the ability to spend enough time solving problems, Erv began to treat his group's paperwork and approval processes as problems to be solved. As a result, he felt slowed by them, questioned their value, and ultimately forced them through his own problem-solving process. His work met the letter of the law, but not the spirit. Yet Erv was more than capable of producing high quality work; he had done so for many years. It was not the tasks themselves that he couldn't do; it was the excessive amount of one task type relative to his internal needs that finally brought him to the point of making inappropriate conversions.

Finally, task type preferences often end up being expressed as "values" by frustrated people. When someone's actual blend is too far removed from his ideal blend, he might begin to devalue the type of task he feels overwhelmed with. During his difficult year, Erv often declared, "All this paperwork is killing our group!" Similarly, someone who feels overwhelmed with too many Long Range tasks might say that "we are doing too much 'strategy' and not enough real work!" Someone who is overwhelmed with Troubleshooting tasks might say that "we do too much firefighting."

Statements like these seem to be about value, but they are really just reflections of an imbalance in task type blend. In these moments, the speaker might truly believe that there is no value at all in one of the task types. In reality, of course, each type has value, and even the most aggravated person will come to see that value when his or her own balance is restored to its measurable optimum blend.

When dealing with others who have a mismatch in their task balance, there might not be a remedy other than simple awareness. If you are in a position to assign or allocate work, then certainly you might have the ability to help correct the situation. If you are in a position to coach or advise the others, you might also have a chance to help them adjust or redefine their own workloads in useful and productive ways. On the other hand, if you have neither the authority to make changes nor the relationship to help another person to do so, you might be relegated to a seemingly powerless position.

Yet even in cases where you cannot fix the situation, there is value in being aware of it. Knowing why a person is "so stressed out" can be enough to help us develop a more empathetic perspective and to be a bit more patient when the inevitable stress behavior comes. Moreover, if you are able to communicate your understanding of his/her struggle, it might help your long-term relationship. Statements such as, "I really respect that you are solving all of these problems as they come up," can be very useful. By honestly acknowledging that the person is over-extended in one of the three task types, you might be able to successfully create a connection and reduce the intensity of difficult interactions. Simply letting someone "vent" to you about how there is "too much of this" or "too little of that" can go a long way toward keeping your relationship on a positive course.

Using Your New Perspective

Think in Blends, not in Absolutes

The good news about tasks as viewed through this new perspective is that all of us have both the capability and need to perform all three types of task and receive all three types of feedback. While it's true that we all have a preferred "blend" of the three types, all of us have need for at least a small amount of each. And while some of our preferred blends favor one or two specific task types, others of us prefer a more equal balance of the three.

Erv Thomas, for example, was being asked to spend more time on Methodical tasks and less time on Quick-Fix tasks than his natural preference required. But even during the years when he was successful and happy at work, he still had some Methodical tasks to complete. Most of us have e-mail, phone calls, and other regular activities each week. It's not that Erv needed "no"

Methodical tasks, just that he needed less of them than what his group unknowingly began to ask of him.

If, in reading through this chapter, you have felt strongly that you don't want *any* of one of the task types, it is probably an indication that you are currently getting too much of that particular type. When you are brought back into balance, you will likely find that there is some of each type of task in your preferred blend.

Change Type When you Change Task

One of the most interesting and useful conclusions from the research into task type is that we can use simple awareness of it to increase satisfaction without changing job responsibilities. If you are beginning to feel bored, dissatisfied, restless, or distracted, this might be an indication that you are in need of a different sort of feedback than you are getting. If you have the freedom to switch gears and work on something else, then there is a simple trick to increase your satisfaction:

> When you are changing tasks because you "don't feel like" doing something any more, be sure that your change of task is also a change of task type.[2]

Imagine that you have been responding to e-mail messages for the past 40 minutes. You are beginning to feel restless and decide to work on something else. You have two choices: You can either take care of some routine paperwork, or you can work on the plan and schedule for purchasing a new piece of equipment for your company. Which do you choose?

Given the choice, you should select the planning work because it is a different task type than the e-mail (Long Range versus Methodical). Regardless of how strong or weak your overall preference for Methodical task perks, your feeling of restlessness indicates that you might have reached your threshold for the moment. If you are able, you might as well make the conscious choice to try something different.

Convert Task Types with Care

When we are not having our needs met in terms of task perks, we might attempt to convert certain task types to others (see Figure 7-1). This type of conversion is a double-edged sword. On the one hand, it can be very helpful to reframe and refocus our activity in terms of the tasks we prefer. When undertaken consciously and with clear intention, this can help to reduce job dread and increase our

level of satisfaction. On the other hand, if we make these conversions uncon-
sciously or haphazardly, we risk becoming ineffective at the work itself, which will
make our jobs more painful and hurt our productivity.

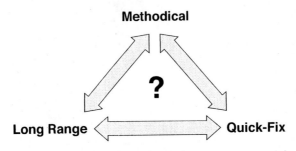

Figure 7-1 *Conversions between the three primary task types are possible but should be
attempted carefully.*

Table 7-1 indicates how it *might* be possible to make conversions between
task types. But beware! If an approach like the one listed under "Try This
Strategy" doesn't work, it is best to stop trying to convert the task type altogether and find a different task to meet whatever task type you need. The approaches under "Avoid This Strategy" should be carefully avoided.

Table 7-1   *Converting Between Task Types*

To Convert From	To	Direction	Try This Strategy	Avoid This Strategy
Quick-Fix	Long Range	⇐	Solve the immediate problem first and then make a plan to prevent it from happening again.	Focus on "the broader issue" as a way to avoid solving the immediate problem.
Methodical	Long Range	⇙	Make a plan for the methodical work that describes what success looks like (the end result).	Allow a huge backlog to build up and then work through it systematically.
Long Range	Methodical	⇗	Make a plan to determine what routine steps are needed to achieve the end goal and then do them.	Ignore the end goal or big picture and focus on the routine activities that are most comfortable.

96

To Convert From	To	Direction	Try This Strategy	Avoid This Strategy
Quick-Fix	Methodical	⬿	Follow a standard, proven troubleshooting process with steps that apply to any problem situation.*	Retreat to the routine that is comfortable instead of fixing the problem.
Long Range	Quick-Fix	⬿	Stand by for any problems that arise; meanwhile, work to fix issues with work flow, plans, and so on.	Wait until things become urgent before starting them, to "create fires to fight."
Methodical	Quick-Fix	⬿	N/A**	Discount, ignore, or hurry through the routine haphazardly to get on to more exciting fix-it or "rescue" scenarios.

*This would be, for example: Step 1. Define the problem; Step 2. List possible causes; Step 3. Prioritize causes by likelihood; Step 4. Test for first possible cause, and so on.

**It is exceedingly difficult to reframe a Methodical task as a Quick-Fix task without adding false urgency or unnecessary time pressure.

This table shows us that Erv Thomas was in an especially bad situation. He needed less Methodical tasks and more Quick-Fix tasks. That particular conversion is almost impossible to do in a productive way.

Set Up for Success

All of us must do some amount of each task type on a regular basis. Whether or not our tasks match our preferences, it is usually in our best interest to do them as effectively as we can. If nothing else, this puts us in a better position to negotiate changes in our jobs or careers later.

One useful feature of this perspective is that it allows us to look at the work we are doing and make sure we are set up for success in doing it. Each task type comes with specific elements that are required for success. When we are starting a new effort or reviewing our performance on an existing one, we can check to make sure we have these elements in place.

So when working on a Long Range task, be sure to incorporate goals, planning, and resources. When working on a Methodical task, be sure to have in place a system and a schedule, and work to create a habit. And, when working on a Quick-Fix task, be sure to understand the relationship between the problem, the reason for it, and the solution.

The Easy-View Summary

You have now read about the basics of the task balance model, the questions you must ask to determine task type, and the conclusions you can draw based on what you discover. The next figure contains the key to how they work.

Reminders:

1. Remember the *Tips for the Journey* (see Chapter 1, "The Trouble with Work").

2. Think in blends, not absolutes.

3. Change type when you change task.

4. Convert task types with care.

5. Set up for success.

Secret 3: The Perspective of Task Balance

Categorizing the work that we do

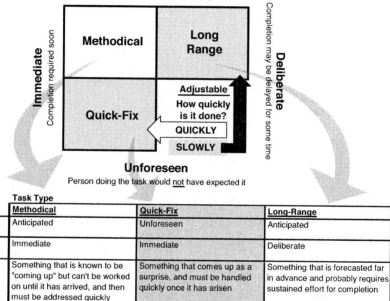

Task Type	Methodical	Quick-Fix	Long-Range
Predictability	Anticipated	Unforeseen	Anticipated
Urgency	Immediate	Immediate	Deliberate
Description	Something that is known to be "coming up" but can't be worked on until it has arrived, and then must be addressed quickly	Something that comes up as a surprise, and must be handled quickly once it has arisen	Something that is forecasted far in advance and probably requires sustained effort for completion
Examples	Responding to e-mail Signing routine forms Entering data	Repairing a PC Responding to a complaint Solving a new safety issue	Building an overpass Planning a software release Revamping a business process
Key Elements	System Schedule Habit	Problem Reason Solution	Goals Planning Resources

Figure 7-2   *Your new perspective: Task balance*

99

Homework: Before, During, and After

Before Work

Before taking your new perspective to work, respond to the following questions:

Consider the three types of tasks: Long Range, Methodical, and Quick-Fix

1. Which of the task types appeal to you the most?

    a. How much of this do you do at work?

    b. In what ways do you do this outside of work?

2. Do you have a strong negative reaction to any of the task types?

    a. In what ways are you required to do these at work?

    b. Do you know anyone who prefers this type of task? Who?

3. Overall, how well do you think your job requirements match your preferred blend of task types?

Bring to mind one to three of your most difficult coworkers and consider the following for each one:

1. Take a guess at which type of work s/he prefers.

    a. How sure are you about your guess? Why?

2. Do you think the person is "well matched" to their job in terms of their preferred task type blend?

    a. What is the basis for your conclusion?

    b. How does your level of match or mismatch compare with his or hers?

    c. How does that person's match or mismatch affect your relationship with him or her?

3. If the person is mismatched, how might you "empathize" quietly? How might you empathize in a conversation with him or her?

At Work

Now it's time to get to work. Do your best to return to your observational state to get the most out of your new perspective today. As you tap your finger on your palm to access your third-person perspective, ask yourself what types of tasks are going on around you.

While you are at work, try to complete the following assignments:

Level 1:

- Pay attention to the tasks you do throughout the day and how much time it takes to do them. Try to determine how much of your day you spend, on average, doing tasks of each type and make note of it.

Table 7-2   *Sample Table for Tracking your Tasks*

Task Type and Key Elements	Time spent in day, on average (%)
Long Range Tasks	
(Goals, Planning, Resources)	
Methodical Tasks	
(System, Schedule, Habit)	
Quick-Fix Tasks	
(Problem, Reason, Solution)	

Level 2:

- Consider your emotions and energy throughout the day. Notice when you are enjoying your work and when you feel your energy levels rise. Notice when you are avoiding tasks, when frustration enters or when your energy levels fall.
- Which task types are you gravitating toward or enjoying the most—Long Range, Methodical, or Quick-Fix?
- Which task types are you avoiding?

EXTRA CREDIT/EXPERT:

- Observe someone near you who has the "perfect job" (in your eyes). Which task types are most frequent or obvious? Which ones are least frequent or obvious? Does that contribute to your view of that job as being "perfect"?

  OR

- Observe someone near you who is obviously dissatisfied with his or her job. Without attempting to fully explain task type, try to make conversation with that person about the kind of work s/he is doing. See if you can empathize with his or her situation.

After Work

After spending the workday using your new perspective, reflect on and/or write about the following topics:

1. Which of the three task types (Long Range, Methodical, Quick-Fix) did you notice yourself doing most often?
2. Which did you notice yourself doing least often?
3. Are there any task types you would like to do more or less frequently in your workday?
4. Did you notice an overall "theme" to your workplace in terms of the type of tasks everyone works on?
5. Are certain task types rewarded more than others where you work? How do these compare with the task types you prefer?
6. Which task types do you think your most difficult coworkers prefer?
7. Is there a difference between their preferred task types and yours? Does this help you to understand conflict between you and them?
8. Did your new perspective help you to empathize with someone else's dissatisfaction?
9. Did it help you to better understand your own dissatisfaction?
10. What else did you see, notice, or learn?
11. What were your two most important conclusions from this section?

Choose a person with whom interaction is difficult. What is the issue? Does task balance come into play? Write about the other person's preferred tasks, your preferred tasks, and how they cause conflict. Is there any action you can take based upon this new information?

Want More?

Want more information about observing, measuring, and learning from task balance? For more stories, exercises, and useful worksheets, visit www.likeworkagain.com/tasktype.

chapter eight

Got Skills?

Millie's Story

"I got so good at playing the violin that they made me the catcher. It almost killed me."

Millie's mixed metaphor is no mistake. She started at the bottom in a beverage bottling company, and over time she got assigned to what seemed like every post in the building. She became so knowledgeable that she represented the factory's concerns on a number of corporate improvement initiatives. Her superiors thought she was ready for management. Who would be better than someone who knew how to do most every job?

Millie's reality was different. Having spent her whole career *doing* things, she was not prepared to get *other people* to do them. "Everything I had ever done worked against me," she said. "My motto was 'get it done.' Now, instead of one station, I was responsible for 20. I naturally assumed that I should be watching all of it, all the time."

"The more I worried about everything getting done, the more I tried to do it all. The more I tried to do it all, the more stress I felt. The more stress I felt, the more I fought with my employees. The more I fought with my employees, the more I worried about everything getting done. The year I spent in that vicious cycle took ten more off my life."

A slightly older coworker aided her escape. "She pulled me aside one day and said, 'I can end your misery if you will let me.' I started to argue but didn't have the energy. All I could say was, 'I didn't realize it showed.' She helped me see that my new goal was the output of the other people, not of their equipment, and that I needed some new skills to succeed. Who knew that 'the ability to influence other people' was a skill? It was news to me."

Fortunately, Millie was a quick learner. With a new perspective on the skills she needed, she devoured books and classes on teamwork and leadership. By being honest with her team about her shortcomings, she was able to reestablish trust with most of them. By the end of her second year, she was a much better supervisor. More importantly, she was a lot less stressed.

Secret 4: Get the Right Skills

Skills Defined

In the classic movie *The Karate Kid*, a wise and mysterious expert teaches karate to a headstrong young man. In the first several "lessons," he directs the young man to wax cars and do other chores using specific hand motions. Only after the youngster rebels against the litany of chores does the instructor finally show his secret: Repetition has trained the protégé to make specific body movements that are pertinent to the martial art. The sensei attacks his trainee with the famous line, "show me 'wax on, wax off,'" and watches with bemusement his student's surprise at his own defensive capability.[1]

What the young man learns, of course, is a skill. "Skills" is a common term in the workplace, and "soft skills" has become a fashionable way to refer to adeptness at interacting with others. When we hire someone new, we try to teach them skills. When we disagree with someone, we cite their lack of job skills or their lack of listening skills. And when we apply for a new job, we work hard to convince our interviewers that we have the skills needed to do the work.

As a result of the plentiful and confusing attention on skills, this arena lends itself to mistakes and misinterpretations. Yet in situations where none of the other three perspectives in this book provide insight, an objective look at skills can be quite helpful.

The progression is important. We started by examining *how* we do things in Chapters 2 and 3, then *why* we do them in Chapters 4 and 5, and finally what things we *like* to do in Chapters 6 and 7. These three secrets—behavior, motivation, and task balance—give us the ability to understand and respond to a wide variety of situations. But sometimes there seems to be something else at play, something still invisible through our three other sets of glasses. That's when we look to skills.

A skill is any talent or ability that can be learned or improved.

Whether it is the bodily movement of a martial art, the intellectual knowledge of computer software, or the interactive finesse of convincing another person to buy something, our skills enable us to be successful at work and at home.

One Simple Question

It is not necessary or advisable to carry around an exhaustive list of skills, nor is it a good idea to spend too much time thinking about whether *other people* have the skills they need (unless their skills are actually your responsibility). When it comes to liking work again, the main skills that matter are yours! And all you need to do to use the secret of skills is to ask one question:

What things could I learn that would help me do this job more easily?

It seems simple, but this question can lead to complicated and useful exploration. There is much more to our skills than meets the eye.

Two Kinds of Skills

Hard Skills

Have you ever wished you were an astronaut? What if your wish came true, and you were to be the lead pilot of a space shuttle mission six months from now? What would you do today? Most likely, you would seek out pilot training, study graphics depicting the control panels, and try your best over the next six months to learn as much as you could about which buttons to push, when, and why.

What you seek, of course, are the skills you need to survive. More specifically, you are seeking "hard skills."

Hard skills consist of objective information that does not vary between the people using it.

Hard skills typically relate to a specific topic. They can consist of abstract, theoretical knowledge, or of practical, concrete methods of action (see Table 8-1). Either way, they do not change depending on who is learning them. As a result, hard skills are usually easy to conceptualize and discuss.

It is easy to list the hard skill requirements for a job and to see when an individual's skills don't match the list. ("Ralph doesn't know how to use the copy machine.") Whether via classroom instruction or on-the-job training, most workplaces provide at least basic hard skill training. Otherwise employees would not be able to do anything! If that training is delivered ineffectively or is not readily available, the situation can certainly contribute to job pain. But hard skill issues are not usually the major factor causing job dread. Because the issues can be identified and discussed easily, they are often resolved quickly.

Table 8-1 *Categories of Hard Skills with Examples*

	Abstract Knowledge	Concrete Implementation
Specific Topic (e.g. flying the space shuttle)	**How it works** (e.g. navigation and electronics system theory)	**How to use it** (e.g. how to take off and land)
Specific Topic (e.g. company accounting practices)	**How it works** (e.g. principles of accounting)	**How to use it** (e.g. how to file quarterly reports)

Soft Skills

Soft skills are a different story. Imagine that you are told to fax a letter to your company's CEO requesting funding to solve a problem. There is a big difference between knowing how to send a fax and knowing how to write a letter! Faxing is objective; the steps are the same for everyone who uses the machine. But effective writing is another story. Soft skills, in this case "written communication," are implemented differently for different people. Two people might both exhibit skilled writing, yet produce very different letters. And two readers might disagree over whether the same letter is, in fact, "well written." It is a lot easier for someone else to determine whether you "know how to" use the fax machine than whether you "know how to" write an effective letter.

Soft skills consist of subjective abilities which vary in implementation between different people.

In the last ten years, work in the field of "Emotional Intelligence" has highlighted a wide variety of such soft skills.[2] Soft skills, like hard skills, can consist of abstract knowledge or of concrete actions. But unlike hard skills, soft skills do not apply to specific topic areas. Instead, they apply more generally to tasks (what gets done), to people (who does it), or to processes (how they do it). As a result, soft skills are more generally applicable, but more difficult to conceptualize and discuss.

Table 8-2 *Categories of Soft Skills with Examples*

	Abstract Knowledge	Concrete Implementation
Task (Skills related to the work itself)	**Understanding Problems** (e.g. the ability to conceptualize an abstract problem)	**Planning for Results** (e.g. the ability to set and act upon goals)
People (Skills related to the people doing the work)	**Human Awareness and Attitude** (e.g. the ability to empathize with others)	**Interaction and Relationship** (e.g. the ability to influence or build rapport)
Process (Skills related to the systems for doing the work)	**Intuition and Awareness** (e.g. the capacity for creativity or clarity)	**Organization and Focus** (e.g. the ability to follow directions)

Though difficult, discussion of soft skills is worthwhile. Many studies have shown that the presence or absence of soft skills drives a host of workplace issues, including satisfaction, morale, and productivity.[3] Anyone who has experienced a manager with poor interactive skills or a senior executive with poor leadership skills knows this; such scenarios ruin both productivity and joy almost immediately.

Although we can benefit from skills in all of the categories shown in Table 8-2, we will tend to "like" some categories more than others. Why? Depending on our preferences for behavior, motivation, and task balance, we will tend to preferentially develop certain skills. Someone who is outgoing and motivated to help other people, for example, will naturally become adept at *Interaction and Relationship* skills. He or she will gravitate toward situations that require them, and practice makes perfect! Similarly, someone who is more detail-oriented and motivated to discover the truth will be more likely to hone the capacities involved in *Understanding Problems*. But whatever our preferences may be, our jobs often require us to stretch beyond our comfort zones.

The alert reader will have noticed that this book itself teaches soft skills. The ability to take the third-person position, analyze a situation, and respond to it based on that information is in itself a soft skill. The ability to do so when an interaction is emotionally charged is an even more challenging one. And the capacity to adjust our own actions out of our comfort zone to meet the needs of someone else is a skill whose mastery can take a lifetime. The effort is well worth it, though; this can help with job dread and lead to positive results in many other areas.

Seeing "Skills"

Henry David Thoreau said that "it is as hard to see one's self as to look backwards without turning around." While his words apply to much of this book, they are most appropriate to the perspective of skills. Few things are more difficult than taking an objective look at our own strengths and weaknesses. For starters, our self-perception is shaped by our unique experiences; it gets clouded by our pre-conceived notions, egos, and insecurities. All of these block our perception of our own abilities.

Even if we avoid our biases, we still are faced with the simple problem that we might not know what we don't know. How could Millie have realized that she needed to learn about "influencing other people" when she didn't even know that such a skill existed?

The answer, predictably, has to do with perspective.

The Eyes of Others

If our own perspective does not allow us to see our strengths and weaknesses, then one way to see them is by using someone else's. In Millie's case, "someone else" was a coworker who recognized her struggle as a supervisor and risked offering to help.

The prevalence of "peer feedback" and "360-degree feedback" in many companies is based on the same notion. Formal processes take many forms but share a consistent basis: seeing ourselves through the eyes of "others." To be effective, these systems must ask for the right information from the right source. They must ask useful questions that will encourage the right people to share what they know. Peer feedback systems that do this can be quite valuable; those that do not will invariably produce useless results.

Of course, you can solicit peer feedback without a structured system. This requires a high degree of trust between you and the person giving the feedback, a low amount of defensiveness on your part, and a forum in which it is safe and appropriate to have the conversation. It also requires a peer who is willing (and able) to identify (and share) useful information in a way that you can understand (and act on) it. Finding a situation that contains all of these elements is extremely useful but can be quite difficult.

Change Your Own View: An Exercise

By now it should be clear that you can change your perspective all by yourself. The next exercise will help you to separate yourself from your usual way of seeing your own skill needs. Again, we strongly suggest that you resist the temptation to skip over parts of this activity. Though aspects of it might seem tedious or silly, rest assured that all of the steps work together to change your perspective.

Think of one or two difficult situations you are facing at work. Perhaps you have tried to solve these problems with the perspectives of previous chapters, but without success. Write your problems down on a clean sheet of paper, leaving some blank space between them.

Now think of a person outside of work that you care about, a friend or loved one. At the top of your list, write "What Makes [Your Friend's Name] Miserable." Make sure that your own name doesn't appear anywhere on the page. Imagine your friend has come to you with this list, and that he or she is experiencing dread and pain at work because of the items on it. Your fondest wish is to see your friend happy, so you want to help him or her to resolve these issues. You have come across similar problems in your own work, so you have some experience on which to base your advice. Below each item on the list, complete the following sentence: "One thing that might help is if you could learn to…"

Remember that you are giving your friend advice, and try to give the most useful and specific advice you can give, without overanalyzing. Some of your ideas might sound good immediately, like "Learn to speak more slowly to your employees." Others might seem to be naïve platitudes, like "Learn to ignore your boss' yelling." Don't worry about that at this stage. Just try hard to make each suggestion an active one, in which your friend learns to do something rather than learning not to do something. Your advice might be "the answer," or it might just be an idea to get your friend going in the right direction.

When you have finished writing, underline the part of each sentence after "learn to…" Imagine that each of these highlighted skills is going to be the basis for a class. Write a one sentence "course description" for each class, so that prospective students know which ones to take. For example, if one of your items is "Learn to ignore your boss' yelling," you could generalize that to "Separating Yourself from the Emotional Outbursts of Others" or perhaps "Dealing with Toxic Interactions." Record your "course descriptions" on a new, blank page.

At the top of your new page, write the phrase "Skills that Might Help Me." This final list is yours again. You have just seen your job through the eyes of your own advisor! If you were able to develop your skills in the areas on your list, they could significantly reduce the biggest pain factors at your job.

Notice that this process focuses entirely on what *you* can learn. Certainly, there are things that other people could do to make your situation better, but you can only control your own approach.

Developing "Skills"

Making the list, of course, is only half of the story. There is little chance that this new information will lead to any changes in your experience unless you take some action. But how can you develop skills whose titles you just finished inventing?

The answer depends not on the items on your list, but on what kinds of skills they represent. Although the number of possible skills is nearly infinite, the types of skills are not. By using the framework in this chapter, you can hone in on the developmental activities that are most likely to help. Like every other model in this book, this one cannot tell you exactly what to do, but it can help you to decide for yourself.

Developing Hard Skills

If your list contains hard skills, figuring out how to improve them is relatively straightforward. The best alternatives for hard skill development include formal or informal training using coworkers, classes, reading material, teachers, mentors, or research. If what you need are facts, then you need only to find out where they are and to go and get them. Whether or not this is possible is a different story, but at least you have identified the avenue toward improving your skills.

Developing Soft Skills

One vice president in a major corporation went back to school for a degree in psychology. This part-time program cost him time and money, but he was willing to make the sacrifice even though his position did not require the formal degree. Why? "The problems I face are all people problems," he explained. "When I think about the skills I need to solve them, it seems like a psychology degree is my best bet!"

Like the vice president's "skills needed" list, yours is probably comprised mostly of soft skills. If any group of skills can help you to like your job more, most likely it will be soft skills. They address people issues, and people issues are often the driving factor behind negative job experiences.[4] The good news is that your list of skills is a lot shorter than the curriculum for an advanced degree in psychology!

Finding a Model

Whatever skill you are struggling to develop, someone else has probably struggled with a similar need. If you can find a way to learn from their experience, you can avoid "reinventing the wheel" yourself.

One great resource is reference materials. If you wish to improve your goal setting, for example, you might find a book that presents a pattern for creating useful goals. Your book might teach you "three steps to create actionable goals," thereby giving you a new way to think about your own goal setting.

Reference materials are not limited to ink on paper. Books-on-tape, video programs, and web-based formats abound. In fact, some of the most effective soft-skill development aids come in the form of audio CDs and computer activities.[5] Often, the problem is not finding *a* book on your topic of interest, but narrowing down to only *one* such book. By starting from your list, rather than browsing the local bookstore for topics of interest, you can make sure that you spend time and energy developing what you need most.

Practicing

Arguably, the most important tool for developing soft skills is practice. As with anything else we learn, mastery requires that we go beyond just thinking about our new skill and actually put it into action.

Practicing a soft skill is basically the same as practicing anything else. It requires a goal, a plan, effort, evaluation, and repetition. Because soft skills are somewhat nebulous, it is often too easy to "lose track of" portions of our practice. If that happens, the practice becomes less effective and might even cease completely.

To aid you in structuring practice for your soft skills, Table 8-3 shows the parallels between soft skill practice and a more common type of practice with which most of us are familiar.

Table 8-3   *Practicing Bicycle-Riding Versus Practicing Goal-Setting*

Component of Practice	Skill "Riding a Bicycle" (Ages 3–5)	Skill "Setting Clear Goals" (Ages 20–70)
Goal	Get down the street without tipping over.	Do a better job of setting goals for myself.
Plan	Pedal with support from parent or training wheels until I'm going on my own.	Learn a new model for goal setting and use it to create two new goals for myself.
Effort	Go! Ride!	Go! Write!
Evaluation	Three minutes later: Did I fall? Was I able to remove the training wheels?	Three weeks later: Did I achieve my goals? Did they help direct my action?
Repetition	Failure? Get band-aid and try again.	Failure? Get ego band-aid and try again.
	Success? Try again now.	Success? Try again now.

This table illustrates why soft skill practice in our adult lives is so much harder to execute than the more traditional skill practice of our childhood. First, the goal is not obvious; if it is not carefully decided up front, determination of "success" is much harder. Second, the timeline for evaluation is longer, and the criteria are more complex; we are more likely to forget to check back or to incorrectly evaluate our results. Finally, we might fail to repeat the process. The child on the bicycle will try again whether he or she succeeds or fails. Adults, on the other hand, are prone to view either outcome as a reason *not* to try again: Either we don't want to repeat a failure, or we feel as though we "got it" and can move on to something else. Both of these instincts defeat the purpose of practice.

By clarifying the five components of practice *in advance*, you are more likely to practice your soft skills in a way that is productive.

Finding a Mentor

Without the help of her coworker, Millie might have spent more time struggling in her new position. There is nothing more effective than learning from someone who already knows what we want to learn. A willing mentor is a direct route to the development you seek. Such an arrangement might be easier to find than it sounds; many talented individuals are willing to play the role of mentor, either to hone their own skills or to "give back" to those around them.

Mentors can come from anywhere: your company, your community, or your network of friends. The arrangement can be formal or informal. The only requirements are that you have some clear agreement up front about the purpose of the relationship, and that you connect with some frequency as you are developing your skills. If you are able to arrange for a mentor for even one of the skills on your list, you might find a very high payoff.

What If I Can't Get It?

"If you can get to where you like your job just four days out of the week, you are doing well." That's one executive's advice to his organization: Don't let the seeming impossibility of perfection dissuade you from making real improvements in your work life.

It is possible that the path toward developing one or more of your new hard or soft skills is not available. Perhaps you need training that your employer is unwilling to pay for, a mentor that does not exist, or there is simply no time to practice. Although this is not the answer you hope for, the information it provides can be just as useful.

First, you must consider whether there is another way to develop what you need. Could you wait for funding, work toward influencing a superior to approve a class, or join an outside organization to receive additional support? Before you "give up" completely, take time to investigate alternatives. Skill development need not happen instantaneously. A slower path to your goal might work as well as a quick one.

Next, consider the worst-case scenario. What if you simply are not able to develop one or more items on your list? How important are those items to your overall job satisfaction and performance? Consider which areas of job pain are most affected by the skills in question. Are there other ways to address those issues? Are there other issues that are more important?

Liking your work is not about perfection or fixing every last concern. As the executive suggests, it is about making useful changes to improve work life. Every single item need not be addressed. The question is not "How can I get everything that I want?" but "How can I make an improvement?"

Using Your New Perspective

Author Martha Grimes said that "We don't know who we are until we see what we can do." The perspective of skills brings us more than just a way to perform better at work; it gives us a new view of ourselves.

Beware of Bias

We are subject to our invisible biases in all that we perceive; when we turn our perceptions inward, the detrimental effect of those biases can be particularly powerful. Our assessment of our own skills is subject to distortion by many of our self-perceptions.

While it is difficult to perceive these biases in action, there are some visible hints that a bias might be at play. Table 8-4 lists these hints.

Table 8-4   *Potential Biases and Clues*

If you Find Yourself...	Possible Bias at Play	What to Do
Adamantly (and emotionally) asserting that you definitely *do not* have a skill deficiency in a certain area.	"Fight it" (Defensiveness)	Step away from the perspective for now; return later with a trusted, neutral advisor. Start by telling him or her about why it has been important in the past for you to have the skill in question.
Worrying that none of your skills are "up to par" and that you are not as talented as "other people."	"Everything is wrong" (Excessive self-criticism)	Make a list of your strongest skills and how they help you every day. If necessary, find someone who can help you to do so.
Feeling that skill development "isn't important" or that you are "talented enough that you don't have to worry about it."	"Nothing is wrong" (Overconfidence)	Consider that *everyone* has both strengths and weaknesses and that to learn something new you must be willing to see something new. Revisit the "skills I need" activity earlier in this chapter.

"Mind Your Own...Skills"

While the rest of this book focused on reading both yourself and others, so far this chapter has been exclusively about your own skills. While the strengths and weaknesses of others might be apparent, they might also be misleading. Moreover, unless you are in a direct supervisory role, chances are you have little control over the skill development of those around you. We focus on our own skills in this chapter because that is where the leverage lies; your best chance to use the perspective of skills to improve your situation is to use it on yourself. Avoid the temptation of advising others as to what skills to develop.

Silently Notice the Skills of Others

That being said, it can be useful to cultivate an awareness of *your perceptions of* the skill levels of those around you. If you suspect that a coworker has strong influencing skills, for example, you might solicit that person's help in deciding how to ask your management for something that you need. By the same token, if you have reason to believe that someone lacks analytical skill, then you might rightly hesitate to rely on his or her calculations in critical situations.

Your ability to accurately assess the skills of others can help you negotiate the daily needs of your work. And because "assessing the skills of others" is in itself a soft skill, the more you practice, the better you will get. The key is to stay aware, use the third-person position, and be open to new information, considering that your initial assessments might not be correct.

Avoid Judgment and Certainty

In cultivating awareness of your skills and the skills of those around you, it is important to avoid attaching either judgment or certainty to your perceptions. We have spoken many times in previous chapters about the dangers of using your new perspectives to be judgmental; it is a guaranteed way to fail if your goal is to enjoy your job. Attributing certainty to your assessments of skills is equally dangerous. True skill levels can be disguised by circumstances; people often seem more or less capable than they really are due simply to the requirements placed on them by jobs and managers.

Steer clear of making skill assessments —especially of other people—in emotional situations. If you perceive a skill deficiency in someone else (or yourself) in an emotional situation, other issues are probably at play. That, after all, is why it is an emotional situation: Your invisible "buttons" are being pushed! Step away from the perspective of skills and try some of the other tools in this book. Examine the situation from the perspective of behavior, motivation, and task balance, and wait for the emotional "smoke to clear." Then return to the perspective of skills and see what it can tell you.

The Easy-View Summary

You have now read about the basics of the perspective of skills and the conclusions you can draw based on what it shows you. The next table contains a summary of the different skill areas. Use the easy-view summary of skills to answer the two questions.

- Where are my strengths?
- Where are my development areas?

Reminders:

1. Remember the *Tips for the Journey* (see Chapter 1, "The Trouble with Work").

2. Beware of bias.

3. "Mind your own…skills!"

4. Silently notice the skills of others.

5. Avoid judgment and certainty.

Secret 4: The Perspective of Skills

Learning what we need to succeed

Table 8-5   *Your New Perspective: Skills*

My Hard Skills

	Abstract Knowledge	Concrete Implementation
Related to A TOPIC	How it works conceptually	How to do something practical
My Strengths	_____	_____
	_____	_____
My Development Areas	_____	_____
	_____	_____

My Soft Skills

	Abstract Knowledge	Concrete Implementation
Related to TASK	Understanding Problems	Planning for Results
Related to PEOPLE	Human Awareness and Attitude	Interaction and Relationship
Related to PROCESS	Intuition and Awareness	Organization and Focus
My Strengths	_____	_____
	_____	_____
	_____	_____
	_____	_____
My Development Areas	_____	_____
	_____	_____
	_____	_____
	_____	_____

Homework: Before, During, and After

Before Work

Before taking your new perspective to work, be sure that you have fully completed the exercise in this chapter to assess what skills you might want to develop. After you have done so, reflect on or write about the following questions:

1. Which (if any) skills on your development list did you already know you needed to develop? Which (if any) were new information?

2. How does your workplace support the development of new skills? How can you access this support system?

3. How does your workplace discourage the development of new skills? How can you avoid these pitfalls?

4. Which one skill on your list would help you the most in making your job more enjoyable?

During Work

While you are at work, do your best to observe your skills and those of others from a neutral perspective. If you find you are feeling strong emotions related to your assessment of skills, tap your finger on your palm as in previous chapters and imagine yourself viewing the situation (including yourself) through a window or on a video camera.

While you are at work, try to complete the following assignments:

LEVEL 1:
- Notice your strongest hard and soft skills. How do your strengths help you in your job?
- Take note whenever one of the skills on your development list would help you. How often does this happen? How much would the skill help?

- Which of the needed skills from your list come up most often? How has simply thinking about them helped you to begin developing them?

LEVEL 2:

- Choose a coworker you work with often. Try to come up with one or two skill strengths that he or she has and one or two skill weaknesses. Don't share these with the other person.

- Observe throughout the day to see if your initial perceptions about that other person change.

EXTRA CREDIT/EXPERT:

- Find someone who is an expert at the soft or hard skills that you would like to learn. Ask if he or she will meet with you regularly and share secrets of success for those skills. See if the person will agree to hold you accountable and provide feedback in no more than two to three skill development areas. Be sure to use the practice model described in Table 8-3.

- If a difficult situation or conflict emerges, look at it through all of the other perspectives first and then consider the soft skills of the people involved. How would a specific soft skill on someone else's part have helped the interaction go more smoothly? More importantly, how could your own soft skills have helped?

After Work

After spending the workday using your new perspective, write about or reflect on the following topics:

1. What hard skills seem to be most important to your job?

2. What soft skills seem to be most important to your job? Are they related to tasks, people, or processes? Are they concrete or abstract?

3. What strengths of yours are helping you the most at work? How might you utilize those strengths even more often?

4. What development areas would improve your job satisfaction the most? How might you develop those skills?

Want More?

Want more information about the types, the measurement, and the use of skills? For more stories, exercises, and useful worksheets, visit www.likeworkagain.com/skills.

chapter nine

A Bird's Eye View

Jim's Story

Jim's downtown office overlooked the city. Arriving early each day, he looked out on a sea of traffic. Most mornings, he marveled at the paradox beneath him: traffic congestion thick on one city street, with nearly vacant conditions just a block or two away.

Sitting just a few feet from a quicker route, the drivers below could see only congestion. Lacking Jim's bird's eye view, they sat and waited in the traffic jam rather than improving their situations.

Some days the situation made him smile with a wry grin: If only they knew what I know. Other days, it frustrated him, and he wanted to tell them. But he had the perspective, and they had the problem, and there was no way to bring the two together.

The Bird's Eye View

Every time you take the third-person position and view a situation as a neutral observer, you take a bird's eye view of your own life. You "hover above," looking at your situation in a new way that provides information about what is happening and what to do about it. Each of the four secrets in this book is like a different video camera, carried with you on your flight, helping you to zoom in on different aspects of what you see.

The perspective of behavior allows you to see "how" you and others work, focusing on the ways in which people interact with each other. The perspective of motivation allows you to see "why" you and others work, looking inside of people at the forces that drive them. The perspective of task balance allows you to see "what" types of work you and others prefer, focusing on the activity itself. And the perspective of skills highlights individual talents, helping you to understand your own capabilities and the capabilities of others.

All of these cameras make you information-rich! Like a commuter armed with an overhead view of road conditions, you consider alternatives that you would not have considered before. The best way to reach your destination might not be the way you would have thought, but small detours in the short run save time, energy, and stress in the long run. Plus, you regain a feeling of control over your situation. The drive gets easier and a bit more enjoyable.

A Still Broader View

When you take a bird's eye view, you get to choose where you put your camera. Jim watched downtown traffic from a tall building. Helicopters and satellites make it possible to go higher, looking at an entire city or an entire country. Each broader position brings with it new information and reveals new patterns.

Your third-person position at work has the same flexibility. In previous chapters, you learned to make fine adjustments during difficult interactions at work. You can adjust your pace here or change your emphasis there to improve relations or get better results in the moment. This is like deciding to try a different road when you learn of a traffic jam.

It is also possible to work at a higher level, using your knowledge to make decisions that have broader and more powerful consequences. This is like choosing to improve your commute by moving to a new neighborhood or a new city. It is this broad perspective that you use when you consider your job as a whole.

The Third Person, Revisited

Our initial exercise with the third-person position involved three sheets of paper. You stepped on and off of numbered pages as you considered a conflict from various sides. You might recall from Chapter 1, "The Trouble with Work," that the "first person" was your own position, the "second person" was the other's position, and the "third person" was the observer role that has since proven to be so important. In the third-person position, you watch a whole interaction as if you were a fly on the wall (Figure 9-1).

Imagine a broadened version of the third person from which you can see all of your interactions at once. In this position, you are like a fly on the wall over your entire job!

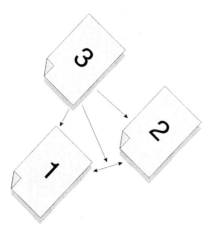

Figure 9-1 *The third-person position and observation/interaction*

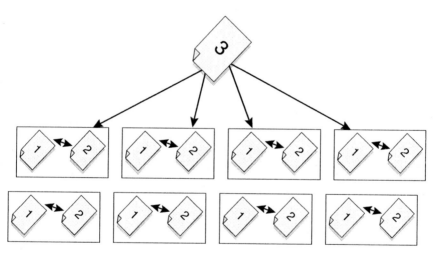

Figure 9-2 *The expanded third-person position*

The expanded third person (Figure 9-2) is the position that is most powerful in creating long-term change in your work life. It is the best position from which to ponder why you dread your job. It is like the position that allows a commuter to go beyond choosing which road to take and consider which city to live in and whether to drive or take the bus.

Sources of Pain

There is an old adage that asks how one goes about eating an entire elephant. The answer, of course, is "one bite at a time." The same is true for any other complicated problem. Anything that seems overwhelming on first glance is best handled in manageable pieces; understanding your job dread is certainly no exception.

Return now to your list of the things that cause you pain at work. Open the envelope and read what you wrote as you read Chapter 1. It is now time to deal with the "whole problem" as you defined it. The first step, of course, is to understand it from the expanded third-person position.

Mary's List	
Problems	**Evidence**
Tommy is so bossy!	Yells, points, argues
I hate voicemail	???
Sue bugs me	Wants to do things "her way"
Mean manager	Criticizes me
	Not helpful

Figure 9-3 *Sample list (repeated from Chapter 1)*

How? Consider for example the "Mean manager" entry in the sample list in Figure 9-3, written by an unhappy worker named Mary. When Mary completed this exercise, her first thought was, "My manager is mean," and her second was,

"I can tell because he criticizes me." Her "problem" was her experience; her "evidence" was how she knew she was having it. Both came as a result of thinking in the first person position: Mary was thinking as "herself" and using sentences that started with "I."

When we invited Mary to consider the same entry from the third-person or observer position, her statements changed. As an observer, she was required to use sentences beginning with "he and she" rather than with "I." As a result, she wrote a new statement: "Because Mary perceives that her manager is criticizing her, she has come to believe that the manager is unkind" (see Figure 9-4).

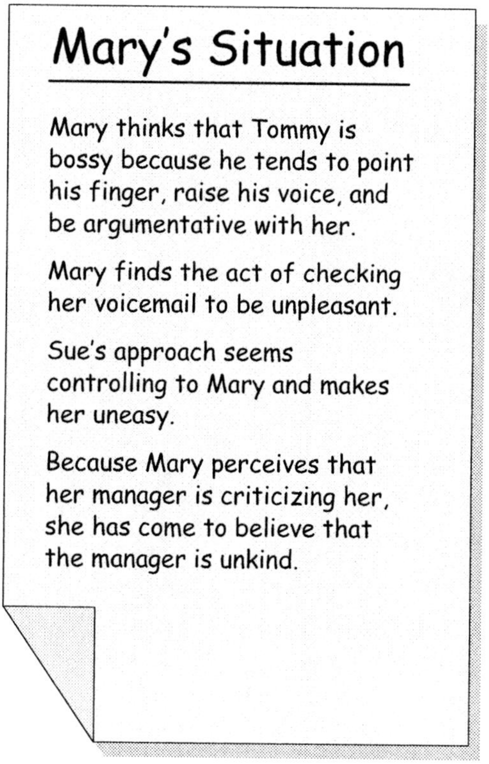

Mary's Situation

Mary thinks that Tommy is bossy because he tends to point his finger, raise his voice, and be argumentative with her.

Mary finds the act of checking her voicemail to be unpleasant.

Sue's approach seems controlling to Mary and makes her uneasy.

Because Mary perceives that her manager is criticizing her, she has come to believe that the manager is unkind.

Figure 9-4   *Change in Mary's interpretation*

Note the powerful difference between these two seemingly similar problem statements! If *I work for a mean manager who criticizes me all the time*, there's not much "I" can do but grin and bear it or give notice and quit. But if *Mary has a belief that her manager is mean because she perceives that he frequently criticizes her*, then a whole new set of questions open up. Why does Mary perceive criticism from the manager? Why is the manager behaving in a way that seems critical? Is it really criticism? Is it really aimed at Mary? What is the content of the "criticism?" What does it suggest about the manager's behavioral style, motivational factors, and preference of task type? What does Mary's strong negative reaction to the supposed criticism suggest about her own behavioral style, motivational factors, or preference of task type? Is there a skill problem here? How might Mary change her relationship with the manager? How might Mary change her interpretation of her manager's actions?

Perhaps the manager is exhibiting directing behavior, which is offensive to Mary's steady behavioral style. Perhaps the conflict is rooted in motivational differences, with the manager striving for power and Mary striving for truth. Perhaps the manager's task balance is causing him stress, and Mary might be able to help by taking over some of his routine work. Notice how framing the "problem" in the third person opens the door to many possible responses.

From the expanded third-person position, Mary is no longer hopelessly stuck in a terrible situation. "I'm stuck here and I hate it," converts to "Here is what is going on, and here is what I might do about it."

Your Pain: An Exercise

Begin your review with a new blank piece of paper. Label it "[Your Name]'s Situation." For each item on your "problems" list, use the information you recorded in the "evidence" column to objectively describe each issue.

Never use "I"; instead refer to yourself by name and describe each item as if you were a detached observer. Don't worry about asking follow-on questions or solving your problems; for now just get your list rewritten.

For example, the first entry in Mary's list (Figure 9-3) might turn into the following: "Mary thinks that Tommy is bossy because he tends to point his finger, raise his voice, and be argumentative with her."

Of course, if you have already resolved an item you listed, there is no need to recopy it. By the same token, feel free to add any new issues that have come up since you first made your list. Your goal is to have a broad overview of your entire situation.

You are like a specialist reviewing your case. Before you can suggest a solution, you must get as complete a picture as possible of the whole situation. If you like, imagine that you are watching yourself at work through a window or from above to help keep yourself in the expanded third-person position.

Your Critical Few: An Exercise

As you were writing, you probably already started thinking about the questions each item raised. By now, you might be worried about the sheer length of your list. Thoughts such as, "Why does he do that?" or "Why do I perceive that?" seem interesting at first, but in sheer volume they soon become overwhelming—a sea of problems. Remember that it is neither possible nor advisable to tackle everything at once. Never try to eat an elephant in one mouthful!

Instead, you must find just a few things to work on. These "critical few" might be the things that cause you the most misery, or they might be the things that are easiest for you to fix. Read over your rewritten list, remaining in the expanded third-person position. First, combine any items that seem similar or related. Working from the expanded third person, you might realize that what seemed like different problems were really just different aspects of the same issue. This helps to find the real causes behind your distress.

Second, circle between one and three items that create the most distress for you. These are your biggest problems. Solving them will greatly reduce the pain you feel at your job. Simply working on them will give you a sense of control over your environment and reduce your feeling of powerlessness because you will be expending your energy for your own benefit.

Finally, underline between one and three items that seem easiest to solve. You might have already worked on them during previous chapters, or perhaps in rewriting them a solution became apparent. These are your easy hits, opportunities to try out your skills and see some quick results. A small success here will give you the reinforcement you need to "keep at it" on a more difficult problem. And a mistake here will bring with it a quick learning opportunity. Small wins are empowering; small losses provide education without delay.

For now, select *one* of your biggest problems and *one* of your easy hits. You have surveyed your entire situation from the expanded third-person position and selected your starting point. From here, you will begin to build a strategy.

Finding Solutions

Interpretation

When you have found your starting point, it is time to dig deeply into the two items you selected. Work with one issue at a time, thinking about it as if it were someone else's problem. Look at it with each of your new perspectives: behavior, motivation, task balance, and skills. Be sure to work in the third-person position, avoiding the use of "I." This exploration might be lengthy and can easily take 30 minutes or more of reflection and writing.

Answer each of the following questions from the third-person position:

- What behavioral issues are involved (Secret 1, page 40)? What actions might help?
- What motivational issues are involved (Secret 2, page 72)? What actions might help?
- What task balance issues are involved (Secret 3, page 99)? What actions might help?
- What skills are involved (Secret 4, page 119)? What actions might help?

While working on a single issue, you will find that some perspectives are more useful than others and that some ideas come up repeatedly. These "themes" are clues in your analysis. You will know you have reached a possible interpretation, or reason for the situation, when you can answer the question, "What is really going on here?"

From Interpretation to Action

Your interpretation is only as good as the action plan it suggests. When you have finished analyzing your situation, you must use your interpretation to come up with a few simple and reasonable actions that you can take in the next few weeks. "What is really going on here?" must lead you to, "What am I going to do about it?"

Remember that your action plan should be *simple*, meaning that you can remember what you are supposed to do, and *reasonable*, meaning that it is possible for *you* to do it. Take care to avoid giving yourself complex assignments and also to avoid assigning action items to other people.

You can only control yourself.

Solutions that involve "getting someone else to do something" are not valid here; the question is only what you will do.

If necessary, return to your interpretation and come up with other ideas until you have a simple and reasonable action plan.

Staying Open

After you decide what to do, there is nothing left but to do it. As you put your new strategy into practice, be sure to stay open to new information and new ideas. None of us are infallible, and difficult situations are by definition the hardest to diagnose. Most likely, your initial interpretation will need revision. Stay open to cues that either your interpretation or your strategy is in need of adjustment. Review the perspectives in this book and your ideas and strategies frequently.

Remember, your goal is to make your difficult situation better. Doing so is hard work and might take sustained effort. The correctness of your first, second, or tenth interpretation of the situation is irrelevant. What matters is the improvement you ultimately make in your work life. Feel free to change, revise, or delete your interpretation and your action plan. If you like, you can write them in pencil or on an erasable board to remind yourself that they are completely flexible.

Should I Stay or Should I Go?

When you wrote your original list of problems, you also noted your thoughts about leaving your job. You thought you would like to stay, or you thought you wished to leave, or perhaps you were not sure. Since then, as you have read this book, you might have changed your mind.

Many causes of job dissatisfaction can be repaired with the tools presented here. The underlying problem might not disappear entirely, but the negative impact can be reduced substantially. No situation is ideal, but many can be made "good enough" or better.

Of course, sometimes a job change is still the best solution. If you are in an abusive, unsafe, or unhealthy environment, a change is obviously warranted.[1] Even in a less overtly dangerous situation, you might not be able to express your passions and skills in a way that meets your employer's business need. If so, a job change might be your best course of action.

Assuming that you are not in imminent physical or psychological danger and assuming that you can use the tools in this book to handle the regular problems of daily work life, the question becomes one of compatibility between you and your job.

Me Versus My Job

In thinking about this question, it is useful to imagine your job as another person. This fictitious individual is neither your boss nor any of your coworkers. It is an imaginary embodiment of the needs, demands, and benefits that your job provides. Why do this? Your job, like any other person, has tendencies and preferences that can be seen through your four new perspectives.

First, your job has certain behaviors that it exposes you to and others that it expects from you. To be successful, which behavioral styles must you exhibit? Do you need to direct, to inspire, to stabilize, or to regulate? Are there behavioral styles which, if you exhibit them, will cause friction or problems?

Second, your job requires that you pursue certain motivational factors to succeed. Does your job require you to strive for Truth, Results, or Power? How about for Assistance, Form, or Structure? Are there factors which, if you strive for them, will cause you to act in a way that is contrary to what your job needs from you?

Third, your job gives you the opportunity to do different tasks. Are there more of one type than another? Do Methodical, Quick-Fix, or Long Range tasks come up frequently? Do any types come up infrequently?

Finally, your job requires that you exhibit certain skills. What hard skills does your job require? What soft skills do you use on a regular basis? Do you have skills that your job keeps you from using? Do you lack skills that your job needs you to have?

Your job's needs and tendencies in each of the four areas might be very similar to, or very different from, your own. The question becomes, "Can my job and I get along?"[2]

Our "Relationship"

Rhonda was ecstatic at the opportunity she had been given. A career middle manager, she was offered the position of Vice President of Human Resources in a small firm. Not only did the position come with an executive title, but with all of the perks associated with it: an office with a view, an expense account, and a dedicated secretary to manage her appointments and files.

Two months later, her demeanor changed. The company was fraught with problems, and they all seemed to land on her desk. "Vice President indeed," she confided in a friend, "A better title would be 'Clean-up Crew for the Person before Me.'"

When two individuals come together, whether as friends, business partners, or life partners, everything might start off looking rosy, but problems can arise quickly.[3] The same is true for a person and a job. The initial euphoric feeling that comes with a new and exciting position is often referred to as the honeymoon period. When that ends, all of us feel at least a little let down. The reality is rarely as good as the fairy tale, and buying toothpaste is far less exciting than buying a diamond ring.

The goal in relationships, of course, is not to be on a perpetual honeymoon, but to find a partner with whom we are compatible over the long term. That way, the ups and downs become a backdrop for a stable relationship, rather than excuses for drama and strife. The same is true of our relationships with our jobs.

As you think about your job as if it were a person, consider how it is compatible with you and how it is not. Is there behavioral conflict between you? Motivational conflict? Task balance conflict? Do your skills complement your job's needs, or are they at odds with each other?

Those with great relationships and those with great jobs agree: It takes work to get there, and there are downs along with the ups. It's not necessary that you be one hundred percent compatible with your job, but it is useful to know how "the two of you" are compatible and how you are different.

No Decision: The Best Decision

There is nothing wrong with deciding that a job change would benefit you, even if it will take years to accomplish the change. Perhaps you have done your part to make the position work, but you just don't fit and are not in the right place. It might be that you and your job are simply not compatible. Your new perspectives will help you find a new position that is more compatible with your fundamental needs and tendencies.

On the other hand, there is nothing wrong with staying where you are. It might be that after years in the same place you simply don't want to leave and would rather work to make things better. Or, perhaps less happy peers have influenced your thinking, and in reality you would be happy if you could just make a small improvement. There's no shame in going, but there's no shame in staying either.

Your best option might be to avoid deciding. Unless you are in physical or emotional danger at work, you can try to make some improvements, cultivate an awareness of the real drivers for your desires to leave or stay, and see if the resulting changes bring with them a shift in your feelings for your job as a whole.

Even as you work to improve your current job, you can also be "looking around" at other options. The more you use your new perspectives, the clearer your picture will become of what you do and don't want in your workplace. You can try to improve your situation as you keep an eye out for something better.

It is both possible and advisable to cultivate a fondness for your current job as you look for a different one.

This paradox brings multiple benefits. First, by making a better life for yourself where you are, you will reduce your risk of suffering from the "any port in a storm" syndrome. If you are so miserable that *anything* else looks good, you might take an equally bad or worse position to escape. If you do, six months later the vicious cycle of misery will repeat again.

Second, many job changes involve salary "negotiations." These might come in the form of actual bartering between you and a hiring company, or they might come from your unwillingness to accept any salary below a certain amount. Either way, they affect your financial health for years to come. If all you want to do is escape, you will accept a salary far below what you are worth. It is far better to "negotiate" when your current alternative is not so bad.

Finally, improving your situation at work will also improve your performance. As you work to repair relationships with those around you and influence them more effectively, there is a good chance that you will achieve more. As you look for your next opportunity, a strong performance improves your qualification as a candidate. You will interview better, and your references will be stronger. Potential employers would much rather hire someone successful and desirable than someone who is trying to escape.

For the Moment

If you can, try to reserve judgment on the question of whether or not you should leave. Instead, work to craft a plan for yourself that involves bolstering your enjoyment and performance where you are, while at the same time staying open to new opportunity. You can always revisit the question of whether you want to leave after you have tried the tools in this book for another month or two.

Taking the Broadest Perspective

You have now learned enough about the four perspectives and how to use them to make a substantial change in your work life. From here, what you do is up to you. As you ponder your next steps, consider the following final pieces of advice.

Use Emotional Cues

Many of us have been taught to avoid or suppress negative feelings. This unfortunate practice robs us of one of our best information systems! Our negative emotions are like warning lights on an instrument panel. They alert us that something is wrong and signal us to take action. Closing your eyes when your car's "low fuel" light blinks on does not give you more gasoline.

On the other hand, staring intently at the indicator light, mile after mile, doesn't create gasoline either. Too often, we dwell on or overreact to our negative emotional indicators. This can set off even more negative feelings, causing a terrible downward spiral of panic and misery. Looking for the next filling station is productive; it works toward solving the problem indicated by the warning light. Worrying about the fuel level, the accuracy of the gauge, the consumption of the car, and the price of oil is not productive. If anything, it distracts from your ability to solve the problem.

You will no doubt feel frustration and other negative emotions as you put the ideas of this book into practice. Your job when this happens is to decide what the emotion is telling you and what you might do differently. Don't avoid negative emotions, but don't get lost in a downward spiral of misery either.

Use the Third Person

All of the exercises in this book share a single theme: the third-person position. The more intense the situation, the more important it becomes to "step out of your own shoes" and view what is happening objectively. You can observe one interaction or an entire system. You take a few days to think something over, a few hours to make some notes, or just a few minutes in the restroom to consider things differently. However you use it, your ability to achieve this perception is the key to gaining new information.

The third-person position can never hurt; it can only help.

As you ponder your own situation, notice where your emotional cues are strongest, and in those areas try hardest to use the third-person position. You will find that you widen your field of options and increase your sense of control over your own life.

Solve the Right Problem

With each of your new perspectives, you should be able to see aspects of your job that are causing you stress. Problems are dynamic; they will change from month to month and even day to day. Get into the habit of using your perspectives on a regular basis to maintain an accurate view of the situation around you.

This accurate view is critical; you cannot solve a problem you do not understand. It has been said by many that once you have fully defined a problem, no matter how complex it is, the solution is obvious.

Defining the problem is often the hardest part.

Your new perspectives help you to see clearly through the complexities of your work life. There might be many "issues" going on around you and many things that you wish were different. Not all of those are actually problems. When you have clearly identified the real problems—the drivers of your misery—solutions will become more apparent.

Remember that nobody is more qualified than you are to solve your own problems, once you have defined them clearly. Be sure to spend enough energy on the definition first so that you end up fixing the right things.

Be Supported

Remember to find support where you can. If you established a support network in Chapter 1, you can expand upon it as you go forward. If you did not, now is a good time to find one! Resources and other ideas are available at www.likeworkagain.com/support. Don't go it alone!

In Closing: Steer Your Own Ship

The longer we feel misery about our jobs, the more difficult it becomes to separate our distress from the reasons for it. We complain to family, commiserate with coworkers, and grow to accept the awfulness of our work as just a part of the scenery of our lives. As the list of "what's wrong" grows, it becomes progressively less clear what is cause and what is effect. Did I always hate my boss, or was it because he didn't support me in my conflict with my coworker? Did I always conflict with my coworker, or was it because that first meeting was so tense? Are all meetings tense, or do I just think so because I dread them so much? Did I always dread meetings, or did it start with the first negative one I had? These questions and others like them become difficult to ask and impossible to answer. Meanwhile the downward spiral circles ever lower.

This book has endeavored to provide tools and approaches to reverse the direction of that descending spiral. A new perspective leads to a new idea; a new idea leads to a new action; a new action leads to a new result; and a new result brings with it a different perspective. It's not that everything gets fixed; it's that something changes. With one change comes the possibility of more.

As you approach your own job, using your new perspectives and acting as the specialist, remember that you are in the driver's seat of your actions and responses. Even if your financial situation requires that you work, the local economy requires that you stay with your current employer, your car's mechanical condition requires that you take the bus, and your company policy requires that you speak in approved phrases, you still have a choice in how you approach the problems and challenges around you. You can always choose to try a different perspective and to adjust your strategy if it isn't working. You can always choose to define what you are looking for and to keep looking for it even as you work to make your current situation better. And you can always choose to treat your emotions as useful information without getting lost in them. The work you do defines you even as it supports you. Its ripple effects touch your loved ones, your colleagues, and your community. You are the one who chooses your actions and responses—*Your work is in your hands.* Let your choices be good ones.

Appendix

The information in this field changes rapidly! For the most recent information, validation studies, more stories, worksheets and aids, and methods of self-assessment, please visit our online appendix at www.likeworkagain.com/appendix.

Notes

Prologue

1. Dilts, Robert B. and Judith A. Delozier,. *Encyclopedia of Systemic Neuro-Linguistic Programming and NLP New Coding.* NLP University Press, 2000.

2. See http://en.wikipedia.org/wiki/The_Little_Engine_That_Could for an account of the classic children's story.

3. "China's Only-Generation Learns Value of Hard Work, April 2006, from http://www.chinaembassy.org.in/eng/zgbd/t245141.htm accessed March 2007.

4. See http://www.magictails.com/creationlinks.html, for example.

5. http://www.wsu.edu:8080/~wldciv/world_civ_reader/world_civ_reader_1/kojiki.html.

6. http://www.dreamscape.com/morgana/oberon.htm.

7. http://www.dreamscape.com/morgana/oberon.htm.

8. "Retirement Only A Breather, Business Wire," December 8, 2005, from http://www.insurancenewsnet.com/article.asp?a=top_lh&id=54702&src=moreover accessed March 2007.

9. See Maslow's Hierarchy for a full treatment of growth needs, http://en.wikipedia.org/wiki/Maslow's_hierarchy_of_needs.

10. Buckingham, Marcus and Donald Clifton. "Now, Discover Your Strengths," *The Free Press*, 2001.

11. For a short, easy to remember story highlighting this point, see "The Rabbit on the Swim Team," at http://www.parentsinc.org/newsletter/sept96/rabbit.html and many other locations.

12. This assertion is more than just intuitive. It has been studied many times, with many conclusions. Studies that adopt carefully crafted definitions of "satisfaction" and "perform-ance" have tended to support the seemingly obvious theory, as long as the individuals involved were dedicated and engaged. See, for example, Demerouti, Evangelia, "Job Characteristics, Flow, and Performance: The Moderating Role of Conscientiousness," *Journal of Occupational Health Psychology*, 11(3), Jul 2006 266-280.

Chapter 1

1. "Manic Monday" by the Bangles, see http://www.afn.org/~afn30091/songs/b/bangles-manic.htm.

2. "The number one prescribed drug in this country are anti-depressants," www.cnn.com/2007/Health/07/09; CDC: Antidepressants Most Prescribed Drugs in U.S., Monday, July 9, 2007, firefox_fam.

3. Dilbert Page-A-Day calendar, 2007.

4. See http://www.modern-psychiatry.com/suicide.htm.

5. A recent SHRM (Society of Human Resource Management) study on job satisfaction concluded that 75 percent of American Employees and 82 percent of American Executives are looking for a new job (2004). In 2005 a Gallup poll reported that 83 percent of workers planned to look for a new job once the economy improved. Gallup more recently reported that 80 percent are already looking.

6. *Gallup Management Journal's* U.S. Employee Engagement Index estimates that only 29 percent of employees are "truly engaged" and that 14 percent of them are actively disengaged and intentionally disruptive. See http://gmj.gallup.com/content/20770/Gallup-Study-Feeling-Good-Matters-in-the.aspx for example.

7. See http://en.wikipedia.org/wiki/Abraham_Maslow and http://en.wikipedia.org/wiki/Frederick_Hertzberg.

8. The number of employees calling in sick with stress tripled between 1996 and 2005 (Data Dome '05).

9. Branham, Leigh. *The 7 Hidden Reasons Employees Leave: How to Recognize the Subtle Signs and Act Before It's Too Late.* AMACOM, 2005.

10. Data Dome Inc. 2005 and American Productivity Audit.

11. Data Dome Inc./U.S. Employee Engagement Index 2005.

12. A recent SHRM (Society of Human Resource Management) study on job satisfaction concluded that 75 percent of American Employees and 82 percent of American Executives are looking for a new job (2004). In 2005 a Gallup poll reported that 83 percent of workers planned to look for a new job once the economy improved. Gallup more recently reported that 80 percent are already looking.

13. Ansary, Tamim. *History's Most Underrated Inventions,* November 2006 from http://encarta.msn.com/encnet/Features/Columns/?article=UnderRatedMain.

14. Goleman, Daniel. *Social Intelligence: The New Science of Human Relationships.* New York: Bantam Books, 2006.

15. Adapted from Robert B. Dilts and Judith A. Delozier,. *Encyclopedia of Systemic Neuro-Linguistic Programming and NLP New Coding.* NLP University Press, 2000, by Mr. J. Michael Bown.

16. These instructions are written such that the reader is standing up, however standing is not a requirement. If you have physical restrictions, three different chairs might be used, or a wheelchair moved between the positions. The important thing is that the reader (1) move from position to position and (2) face the other positions as directed.

17. Dilts, Robert B., and Judith A. Delozier,. *Encyclopedia of Systemic Neuro-Linguistic Programming and NLP New Coding.* NLP University Press, 2000.

18. This might not be because of a mistake on your part. If, for example, you are interacting with a person with serious clinical issues, your actions may not produce the intended results. See, for example, *The Sociopath Next Door* by Martha Stout. Broadway Books, 2005.

19. According to many, including Pulitzer Prize winning author Taylor Branch. See *Taylor Branch: We Learn Best Through Stories*, Amy Pickett, ALA Cognotes, June 2004, from http://www.ala.org/ala/eventsandconferencesb/annual/an2004/cognotes-Issue4.pdf accessed Mar 07.

Chapter 2

1. Our fascination with our own behavior and the behavior of others goes back as far as 400 BC; since then a huge number of models of understanding have emerged. Coming from many fields, these models run the full spectrum from the simple to the complex. Some of the most well known, like Myers-Briggs and MMPI, are based on psychology and require weeks or months of study for mastery. But complex models are difficult to apply at work, and some have been shown to be inappropriate in terms of what is measured. See *Employers Face Risks with Use of a Personality Test*, Kaja Whitehouse, Dow Jones Newswires, July 18, 2005, http://www.careerjournal.com/hrcenter/articles/20050718-whitehouse.html, accessed July 21, 2005.

2. Marsten, William Moulton. *Emotions of Normal People.* Routledge, Reprinted 2001

3. Bonnstetter, Bill J. and Judy Suiter. *The Universal Language DISC.* Target Training International, 1993–2004.

4. Ibid.

Chapter 3

1. Bonnstetter, Bill J. and Judy Suiter. *The Universal Language DISC.* Target Training International, 1993–2004.

2. See www.likeworkagain.com/behavior for more information.

Chapter 4

1. In your local bookstore you can find business texts claiming to teach the reader techniques to be a better motivator shelved side by side with others that warn that the motivation of another can not come from you, but only from within. For example, see Bruce, Anne. *How to Motivate Every Employee (Mighty Manager)*, Mc-Graw Hill, 2006, versus Chandler, Steve and Scott Richardson *100 Ways To Motivate Others: How Great Leaders Can Produce Insane Results Without Driving People Crazy*. Career Press 2004.

2. The Task-People-Process framework is useful in other situations. If you are struggling with the solution to a problem, it can be helpful to determine what aspect of the problem really needs solving. A coworker's constant tardiness in returning from lunch, for example, could be due to the fact that he has medical appointments conflicting with his lunch hour (Tasks), is simply indifferent to the issue of his tardiness (People), or has poor time management skills (Process). Each of these causes would dictate a different approach in attempting to solve the problem.

3. Bonstetter, William. *If I Knew Then What I Know Now*. Forbes Publishing, 1999.

4. Ibid. Definitions of the six factors are adapted from Bonstetter.

5. In the original research, those exhibiting this motivational factor were often closely linked with political situations and ambitions. But the definition has since widened. The context need not be political, so long as the goal is authority, possibly over others but definitely over self. Spranger, Eduard *Types of Men*. Johnson Reprint Company, 1966.

6. Form-passionate is the least common type in the U.S.; Bonstetter, William. *If I Knew Then What I Know Now*. Forbes Publishing, 1999.

Chapter 5

1. See www.likeworkagain.com/motivation for more information.

2. Sophisticated instruments that measure motivation have many gradations and combinations of the factors described here. Even so, there are subtleties between individuals that can't be captured. See www.likeworkagain.com/motivation for more information.

3. Lencioni, Patrick. *The Five Dysfunctions of a Team: A Leadership Fable*. San Francisco: Jossey-Bass, 2002.

Chapter 6

1. Feedback is a favorite current topic in both business and education. We hear the word often in the workplace, typically used as in the American Heritage dictionary definition: "The return of information about the result of a process or activity; an evaluative response." But the same dictionary also lists the following meaning for feedback: "The return of a portion of the output of a process or system to the input." This is the type of feedback we are discussing here. If you've ever winced at the screech made by an audio speaker when a microphone is placed too close, you've experienced a painful form of the more technical definition.

2. Gazzara, Kevin. "The Relationships Among the Mixture of Task Types, Performance, Satisfaction, and the Implications for Flow." University of Phoenix Dissertation Thesis, March 2003.

3. This "self-encouragement system" seems to be a big part of what compels us to persevere when things get difficult. That's why we see some managers and trainers almost obsessed with "recognition"—by turbo-charging an employee's internal encouragement with external kudos, managers seem to be able to create more productive and happier employees.'

4. Gazzara, Kevin. "The Relationships Among the Mixture of Task Types, Performance, Satisfaction, and the Implications for Flow." University of Phoenix Dissertation Thesis, March 2003.

5. Daniels, William R, *Breakthrough Performance*, ACT Publishing, 1995.

6. Ibid. Modified version presented here.

7. Kerzner, Harold. *Project Management: A Systems Approach to Planning*, 8th ed. Hoboken, N.J. : John Wiley, 2003.

8. Much has been written about structured approaches to problem solving. For example, see Chang, Richard Y. and P. Keith Kelly. *Step-By-Step Problem Solving: A Practical Guide to Ensure Problems Get (And Stay) Solved*. Jossey-Bass, 1999.

Chapter 7

1. Visit www.likeworkagain.com/tasktype for more information about how this can be measured.

2. Gazzara, Kevin. "Using Task Quotient (TQ) to Maximize Individual Motivation and Job Satisfaction," IEEE Engineering Management Conference, University of Texas at Austin, August 2004.

Chapter 8

1. *The Karate Kid,* written by Robert Mark Kamen, directed by John G. Avildsen, Delphi Films, 1984.

2. One of the defining works in this space was Goleman, Daniel. *Working with Emotional Intelligence.* New York: Bantam Books, 1998.

3. Muzio, Ed, Deborah J. Fisher, Erv Thomas, and Valerie Peters. "Soft Skill Quantification (SSQ) for Project Manager Competencies." *Project Management Institute Journal,* June 2007.

4. Branham, Leigh. *The 7 Hidden Reasons Employees Leave: How to Recognize the Subtle Signs and Act Before It's Too Late.* AMACOM, 2005.

5. For more information see www.likeworkagain.com/skills.

Chapter 9

1. Abuse takes many forms. Thus it can be difficult to distinguish between an unsafe environment and one that is merely unpleasant. See www.likeworkagain.com/appendix for more information.

2. See www.likeworkagain.com/support for resources to help you find areas of compatibility and incompatibility with your job.

3. See, for example, Gaster, Chuck and Eric Gaster. "The Honeymoon Period, a Manager's Tale." *The Journal for Quality and Participation*, Spring 06, http://findarticles.com/p/articles/mi_qa3616/is_200604/ai_n17172795.

Index

FINANCIAL TIMES

In an increasingly competitive world, it is quality
of thinking that gives an edge—an idea that opens new
doors, a technique that solves a problem, or an insight
that simply helps make sense of it all.

We work with leading authors in the various arenas
of business and finance to bring cutting-edge thinking
and best-learning practices to a global market.

It is our goal to create world-class print publications
and electronic products that give readers
knowledge and understanding that can then be
applied, whether studying or at work.

To find out more about our business
products, you can visit us at www.ftpress.com.